A Primer on Nonprofit PR

If Charity Begins at Home...

Kathleen A. Neal, APR

Pineapple Press, Inc.
Sarasota, Florida

This book is dedicated to Arch Beckleheimer, my college English professor, who nourished my love of words, introduced me to Vivaldi, and told me not to get a teaching certificate "to fall back on."

Inquiries should be addressed to:

Pineapple Press, Inc.
P.O. Box 3889
Sarasota, Florida 34230

www.pineapplepress.com

Library of Congress Cataloging-in-Publication Data

Neal, Kathleen A.
    A primer on nonprofit PR : if charity begins at home— / Kathleen A. Neal.— 1st ed.
            p.   cm.
    Includes index.
    ISBN 1-56164-229-0 (pbk. : alk. paper)
        1. Public relations. 2. Nonprofit organizations—Public relations. I. Title.

HD59 .N36 2001
659.2—dc21

                                                                        2001021526

First Edition
10 9 8 7 6 5 4 3 2 1

Design by Shé Sicks
Printed in the United States of America

■ ACKNOWLEDGMENTS ■

There are many people who helped make this book a reality. Spring Asher of Speechworks in Atlanta encouraged me early on. Jackie Erney, public relations professor at Georgia Southern University, went a bit further—begging me to finish the book so she could use it as a textbook. My mentor and friend Ann Watson critiqued early drafts of the manuscript and made valuable suggestions to make it better. Chris Spragg indulged my paranoia and kept updated computer disks containing the manuscript at her house "just to be safe." Anne Isenhower, my "adopted" daughter, kept my spirits up and supported me during some tough times. A special thank-you to my mother, Mary Neal, who cheered me on, and to my sister, Linda Goodyear, who gave me the benefit of her experience as a textbook author. And, of course, my son, William, who suffered through it all and finally said to me, "Thank God you've finished that book. You've only been talking about it for ten years!"

I was also encouraged by the numerous people who wanted a chapter or two to use for themselves even before publication: people from my church who were involved in events at their children's schools; a small but growing nonprofit organization that realized the need for public awareness and couldn't afford to hire a PR professional; and others who found themselves in need of information on how to generate publicity. They cemented my belief that this book will fulfill a big need for a diverse audience.

Finally, I want to thank everyone at Pineapple Press. They saw the potential and supported me through the process. They also kept me straight when my imagination got a little out of whack. Thanks to them, what you won't see in this book is the Association of Similar Syndromes (A.S.S.) holding a special event barbecue called an "Assbecue!"

■ TABLE OF CONTENTS ■

▪ INTRODUCTION ▪

This book is intended to make life easier for those people who find themselves responsible for the public relations efforts of a nonprofit organization. Whether the title is communications director, publicity chairman, community relations coordinator, or information manager, you know who you are. This is *not* the book you should use to study for the Public Relations Society of America's accreditation exam. This *is* the book you should use if you work for the Association of Similar Syndromes and your acronym spells A.S.S. and you need to conduct an image campaign.

The first thing I want you to do is repeat the term "public relations" five times. Why? Because many nonprofit organizations are afraid to use that term. It's as if admitting that your agency has a "PR person" may conjure up negative images for your constituents.

Unfortunately, there are some negative images swirling around the profession. Public relations practitioners bristle at classified ads that read "Public Relations: If you are good with people and have your own car, we have a public relations job for you." I once advertised for a public relations manager and received over 350 resumes from one ad in the Sunday newspaper. Admittedly, the ad was placed in a big city paper, but that number still amazes me! One gentleman wrote a glowing cover letter in longhand on yellow legal pad paper informing me that because he had been raising purebred dogs for ten years, he knew he could work well with people. I never quite made the connection between dogs and PR, but I do know that public relations is not merely the ability to work well with people.

Some media folks immediately put their guard up when "PR types" contact them because they have been burned by the unprofessional actions of a few people. Badgering reporters, sending them cutesy gimmicks or threatening them in any way is *not* how professional public relations practitioners work!

Public relations is a serious discipline. I believe there are three main branches of the profession: agency public relations, corporate public relations, and nonprofit public relations. They all use basic PR tools, but they may use them in different ways. All three branches share the same goals: to inform the public about their service, product, or point of view, and to establish and maintain a good image for their organization. There are many reasons to inform the public about an organization. For nonprofits, it is usually to encourage people to volunteer, give money, support lobbying efforts, disseminate information, or buy into strategies for change.

Nonprofit public relations has no basic element or quirk that makes it radically different from other PR efforts. In some ways it is easier because the media is often more responsive to a nonprofit public relations representative than to a corporate or agency person, whom they may view as trying to get "free publicity." On the other hand, nonprofit PR can be more difficult because of a chronic lack of resources—like money and staff!

For far too long, many nonprofits, especially smaller ones, have not put any resources into public relations efforts, or, if they have, that is the first place they cut back when the budget needs to be balanced. It astounds me that nonprofit boards of directors consisting of successful business professionals do not see the same value in a dedicated public relations strategy for the nonprofit as they do for their own businesses. Yes, nonprofits have to operate in the public interest, but good PR strategies should enhance the public interest and actually be cost-effective in the long run.

So, for whatever title you may have—or want to have when you get out of school—this book is offered as a compilation of thirty years of experience in nonprofit organizations. This book should take you from wringing your hands over the prospect of writing a press release to successfully moving your organization forward by using solid public relations techniques.

What *Is* Public Relations?

· 1 ·

April is Child Abuse Prevention Month. For several years, one city's zoo held an awareness day for a child abuse prevention agency in conjunction with a local television station. It was a day to call attention to and focus on programs the agency provided and to distribute educational information about a serious topic in a fun, nonthreatening environment. A local beauty queen had contacted the agency with an offer to help. She was assigned to stand outside the admissions gate and distribute special discount coupons to visitors.

The morning of the event dawned gray and blustery. It was extremely cold for April. Workers arrived bundled up and went to their assigned areas. The beauty queen was late. When she finally did arrive, she was wearing a fur coat. Zoo officials were horrified but quickly convinced the young beauty to shed the fur and wear a zoo parka for warmth. The fur was safely stored in the security office. What message would it have sent zoo visitors to be greeted at the gate by a young woman wearing a coat made out of animal fur? This was a public relations problem.

So, what *is* public relations? That may be the hardest part of the job—convincing people what it *is* and what it *isn't*. There is no easy answer.

In the book *Effective Public Relations* by Cutlip, Center, and Broom, there are several definitions—some conceptual and some operational. There is the "Official Statement on Public Relations" adopted by the Public Relations Society of America in 1982. There is also a definition that is both conceptual and operational that reads: *"Public relations is a distinctive management function which helps establish and maintain mutual lines of communication, understanding, acceptance and cooperation between an organization and its publics; involves the management of problems or issues; helps management to keep informed on and responsive to public opinion; defines and emphasizes the responsibility of management to serve the public interest; helps management keep abreast of and effec-*

tively utilize change, serving as an early warning system to help anticipate trends; and uses research and sound and ethical communication as its principal tools."

Didn't that just clear it right up for you? And how is marketing different from public relations? And where does advertising fit in (and when should it fit in) for a nonprofit? And what about community relations, or development (which is a nice term for fundraising)? Is this all part of public relations? Is public relations communications or publicity?

I tried to call the regional office of a major chain variety store and got one of those telephone menu systems—you know, if you have a question about your bill, press one. . . . I wanted the public relations department. The "dial by name" option didn't work for me because I didn't know the name of the person in charge of the public relations department. Finally, in desperation, I just pressed numbers until I got a human being—in the shipping department. He had no clue if there was even a PR office in the company. That company has a public relations problem.

So, is public relations also monitoring what your volunteers and supporters hear when they call in on the telephone? If your agency is lucky enough to still have a live human operator, is he or she pleasant to callers? Do staffers at your organization send information when they say they will? If not, what does that communicate? People remember and talk about negative experiences much more than they share positive experiences.

- If you work for the American Lung Association and staff members stand outside the main lobby of the building to smoke . . .
- If your agency is dedicated to environmental issues and the staff doesn't recycle at work . . .

You get the picture.

There was a very good column in *Tactics*, the newsletter for the Public Relations Society of America (PRSA) in November 1997. I share it on the next page with the permission of its author, Florida International University Professor Bill Adams, APR, Fellow PRSA.

COLUMN BY PROFESSOR BILL ADAMS ON THE DEFINITION OF PUBLIC RELATIONS

Q: I've seen a number of definitions for public relations. Does an "official" definition exist?

A: Don't feel alone in your bewilderment over an "official" definition of public relations: No such thing exists. In fact, the field has redefined itself innumerable times since Edward Bernays described public relations as **"information given to the public, persuasion directed at the public to modify actions and attitudes, and efforts to integrate attitudes and actions of an institution with its public and of publics with those of the institution."**

Heavy stuff, but one would expect nothing less from a public relations pioneer who was the first to link the field with behavioral sciences.

By the late 1940s, Phil Lesly had written that public relations **"tells (a) group what others think of it; it helps the group determine what it must do to get the good will of others; it plans ways and means of winning that good will; and it carries on activities designed to win it."** Now here was a definition featuring a planning function, along with reinforcing the two-way nature of the field.

Since then, there have been a number of official and quasi-official PRSA committees responsible for creating a universally accepted definition. One such effort was commissioned by the Foundation for Public Research and Education in 1975. In that study, sixty-five public relations leaders analyzed more than 470 different definitions. The result was an eighty-eight-word sentence that described public relations as a management function for the first time. Five years later, PRSA chartered a special task force that pared the definition down to twenty-seven words and focused on the "mutual" adaptation of organizations and their publics.

But, arguably, the definition with the most staying power was proposed by Denny Griswold, former editor and publisher of *Public Relations News*. It succinctly identified and isolated key components of the field: **"Public relations is the management function which (sic) evaluates public attitudes, identifies the policies and procedures of an individual or organization with the public interest, and plans and executes a program of action to earn public understanding and acceptance."**

In her own inimitable fashion, Griswold had wallet-size cards printed with the definition on one side and her name and contact information on the other.

I still carry the card. ∎

From *Tactics,* the newsletter for the Public Relations Society of America (PRSA), November 1997. Reprinted with permission.

Even public relations professionals can be confused about the precise meaning of the term. As with many components of the profession, it may depend on whom you ask. One component of media relations, for example, is how or if you should follow up on press releases that have been sent out. Pose the following question to two PR practitioners: "Should you follow up a press release with a phone call to be sure the editor received it?" One PR person will say that *yes*, you should always call and ask if it was received, and the other will say *no*, editors don't like that. Neither one is right or wrong. Some editors don't like phone calls, but some editors appreciate the reminder. Don't ask the public relations professional—ask the editor! The point is that if PR people can't agree on that point, how can we expect them to accept one, definitive, easy-to-read-and-understand definition of the term public relations?

There are many public relations objectives for nonprofit organizations, including (but certainly not limited to):
- Creating public awareness
- Recruiting volunteers and members
- Fostering public education about an issue or health concern
- Encouraging attendance at performances, meetings, events
- Creating and maintaining a good reputation

I don't believe fundraising is a direct public relations function. I do think, however, that creating solid, ongoing public awareness about an organization will do nothing but help fundraising efforts by putting a base of knowledge out there in the public domain. The reality is, however, that in many nonprofits, both public relations and fundraising activities are, of necessity, handled by the same person or department.

Consider the Association of Similar Syndromes (A.S.S.). While doing fine work, A.S.S. has been the butt of jokes for years (pun intended). National comediennes have targeted A.S.S. with terrible jokes ("When they say the end is in sight, they mean it!"). The jokes and innuendoes have hurt the organization's ability to raise funds for patient assistance and research. Negative perceptions have hampered media relations and affected staff morale. This is a public relations problem that could be remedied by changing the name of the organization to the Similar Syndromes Foundation (S.S.F.) and launching an aggressive media campaign to rebuild its reputation by focusing on the serious research being done to search for a cure and create better treatment regimens for patients.

I will not be so presumptuous as to offer the perfect definition of public relations. It isn't "working well with people" and it isn't meeting in secret little sessions to determine how to make a board of directors' election go the way you want. It isn't sending flowers to a reporter you want to convince to write a feature story and it isn't dressing like a snail and crawling down Main Street to get news coverage for Save the Snails.

It *is* about presenting your organization to the public with honesty, integrity, and effective methods of communication. It is also about listening to what the public thinks about your organization and taking action to change negative perceptions.

In this age of increased "noise," it can be a challenge to make the voice of your agency heard over the roaring surf of the Internet, the flood of daily faxes, full voice mail boxes, and TV and radio news that feature murder and mayhem. I hope this book will help you get "out of the box" to think about how to use effective, public relations tools to accomplish the good work of your nonprofit organization.

■ Public relations is about presenting your organization to the public with honesty, integrity, and effective methods of communication.

What Do I *Really* Want?

· 2 ·

While working for a nonprofit science museum that depended on ticket sales for over half of its operating revenue, my PR plan included low- or no-cost ways to promote the museum. When the morning crew of a local radio station embarked on a promotional stunt to "Meet Every Listener," I incorporated that into my plan. The measuring stick for success of this effort would be free airtime (during morning drive time) on a popular radio station.

The two deejays arrived after their morning show ended to meet the staff and then "play" with the hands-on exhibits on the museum floor. Fabulous audio was recorded while the deejays cavorted in the traveling exhibit area, talked to museum visitors, and generally had fun. They decided they wanted to have their hair stand on end as part of a demonstration about electricity. A museum staff member had already set up the demonstration for a group of children, so the deejays simply joined the group to serve as the volunteers for the hair-raising segment.

All went well until the soundman moved in really close so he could record the conversation during the demonstration. The deejays were standing with their hands on a generator that creates static electricity. The radio station's mike was mounted on a metal pole. Now, static electricity really prefers metal over human beings, so the electric spark arced from the deejays over to the mike, traveled down the metal pole into the earphones, through the soundman's body, and out through his toes. It was not enough current to hurt him, but it certainly scared him. The next morning all the wonderful audio that demonstrated what fun people have learning hands-on science at the museum was not what played on the radio. Instead, the loud pop that occurred when the spark jumped to the metal pole was played over and over again with accompanying jokes about how "Mr. Science" tried to kill the soundman. I got free airtime on the radio during morning drive time, but it wasn't exactly what I had envisioned.

It is important to identify the public relations goals for your nonprofit organization. What do you really want—what do you really think public relations can accomplish for your agency? Start the process of implementing a PR program plan by stating your objectives clearly. Then, write down strategies for reaching them. Have your executive director and the board of directors review your objectives and strategies and sign off on them so everyone in your organization is on the same page.

Once you have goals and objectives nailed down, you can write a comprehensive PR plan that details the agency's specific goals and spells out how to achieve those goals through public relations activities. Your plan will need to include a method for evaluating success (see Chapter 9: Why Should I Evaluate My PR Efforts?). You can create a yearlong plan or a project-based plan.

I can see you scratching your head and saying, "I don't know what my objectives are and I don't have a clue what strategies to use." That's okay. This chapter is set up to help you understand the process involved. So, let's write a PR plan!

The Similar Syndromes Foundation (S.S.F.) has established a goal to increase volunteer recruitment for the next fiscal year. Using good public relations techniques, the staff plans to assist the agency's volunteer coordinator in reaching this goal. See box on pages 8–9 for S.S.F.'s project-based plan.

That is the basic idea of a PR plan designed for a specific goal or objective. Adding target dates for accomplishing each action item will help keep the plan on track. And, as you progress through the plan, there may be pieces of it that don't work because of time, budget, and personnel. This S.S.F. volunteer recruitment plan is fairly ambitious. There just may not be enough staff, volunteers, or funding to hire temporary workers to complete all elements of the plan. Understand that it isn't written in concrete—you can add to it or change it—but there is something about putting the plan on paper that gives it definition and helps motivate staff to action. Planning and evaluation are essential PR tools for any nonprofit agency. It is important to get into the habit of practicing good planning techniques.

What if your agency wants to enlist the aid of local voters to create or change a law? Your goal is to motivate the constituents of local or state lawmakers to understand that the voters who put them into office want the law created or changed.

■ Planning and evaluation are essential PR tools for any nonprofit agency.

SAMPLE PROJECT-BASED PLAN

Goal   Recruit 20 new S.S.F. volunteers per quarter to attend training. Retain 12–15 of these volunteers for at least one year.

Method

Media   Write and distribute community calendar notices for daily and (strategy) weekly newspapers, appropriate periodicals, and radio stations.

      Schedule appearances by a current volunteer and an S.S.F. staff person on all radio public affairs programs and any local television talk shows.

      Approach a local media celebrity and ask him/her to become a volunteer with S.S.F. for at least one day to write about the experience in the newspaper, prepare a video-taped segment for TV, or report about the experience on radio.

Direct Mail Create a mailing to send to retirement centers that details volunteer opportunities for seniors.

      Contact big corporations that have volunteer programs for their employees (large utilities, banks, etc.) and provide information on volunteer opportunities, especially one-day events (like a fix-up day at your facility) where volunteers from local businesses can participate as a group.

      Mail to schools that have service clubs—both colleges and high schools—to provide information on age-appropriate volunteer opportunities.

Speakers Train volunteers (with staff backup) to speak at clubs (i.e., Rotary, Kiwanis, Jaycees, Garden). Contact clubs to let them know speakers are available. If your agency provides support and research for a disease, have a survivor of that disease be a part of the presentation. If you represent a botanical garden, take seedlings to distribute to the audience.

Develop a model for a speech presentation that is unique and different. Try visually demonstrating how a volunteer's hours mount up by using marbles or pennies in a jar.

Special Events S.S.F. is headquartered in a large city where there are trade shows, a Christmas product show, a family computer show, and a craft fair at area convention centers and shopping malls. Contact the organizers of these shows to see if S.S.F. can have a free booth to distribute information about volunteer opportunities.

Print paper stickers for your volunteers to wear whenever they are on duty that read, "Ask me how to volunteer" or "Our volunteers have more fun!"

Resources
  Budgets Detail which departments' budgets will be used for printing, postage, staff salaries, supplies, etc.

  Staff Decide what tasks can be accomplished by existing staff and volunteers, and which areas may need temporary workers or consultants.

  Contacts Look carefully at board members, volunteers, media, and friends of the agency to determine who can help open doors in the community to accomplish your goals.

  Evaluation Successful recruitment and retention of volunteers is the S.S.F. goal. Assuming that the goal was achieved because you used good PR techniques and worked hard, ask yourself the following questions: How did that success happen? What worked and what didn't work? You need to evaluate your efforts to determine which efforts produced results. At the volunteer orientation ask each new recruit to fill out a questionnaire to determine which of your PR efforts were the most effective.

Use statistics to determine where your new volunteers come from:
  • Do they all live in one zip code area?
  • Are they all within one specific age range?
  • Do they all have a relative with S.S.F.?
Study these kinds of stats to glean information that will make your next recruitment drive more focused, less time-intensive, and more successful. ■

For example, a state child abuse council tried to get a law on corporal punishment changed. In that state, teachers were allowed by law to spank unruly children. Child abuse experts contended that hitting children did no good, only harm. In a Bible belt state, this was a hot issue because the Bible says, "Spare the rod and spoil the child." Parents didn't want the state telling them how to discipline their children. The council asked prominent theologians to write a paper on what "spare the rod" actually meant in biblical times, which was quite different from the modern day meaning. (It actually meant to guide children with a rod—like sheep—not to hit them.) Further research found a law on the statutes that it was a felony to hit a police dog. Citizens could go to jail for hitting a police dog, but teachers were allowed by law to hit a child. Publicizing these facts made a difference, but it didn't get the law off the books. The state decided to retain the corporal punishment law but did allow local school systems the option of implementing it or not. The result was that a significant number of local school systems actually did stop allowing teachers to spank or otherwise strike children.

Just because your organization believes a particular goal is the right thing doesn't mean everyone will embrace it. That's when public relations is most challenging. The goal is best accomplished by providing honest facts that will persuade people to listen to (and hopefully adopt) the position you are promoting. If they don't, all is not lost, because your PR efforts have raised awareness and may have made small adjustments that will help pave the way for future change.

Having individual program or project goals with accompanying PR plans is helpful, but a plan for the entire year is important. A master plan will provide guidance and a timetable throughout the year. It can be a useful tool to show your board of directors what a dedicated public relations plan can accomplish for the organization, and it can help rationalize budget allocations for public relations activities.

Here is a sample yearlong plan for an agency working to eradicate a specific disease. This sample plan is intended to get you started in the right direction so you can build your own public relations plan. With information specific to your organization, you can create a plan tailored to your goals and objectives. It is also important to include target dates for completion of tasks in the plan. Keep in mind that once you have digested other information in this book, it should be easier for you to create a PR plan. I believe that the best basic advice is to create a plan for your organization that will accomplish what *you* want through projects that will also give the media, corporate partners, and the public something *they* want.

A master plan will provide guidance and a timetable throughout the year.

■

SAMPLE YEARLONG PLAN

Goal
Increase public awareness about the disease.
Encourage early detection and treatment of the disease.
Support fundraising for research.

Method
Media

Prepare regular press releases and media updates about advances in research and treatment.

Contact the health reporter at the nearest daily newspaper and request a meeting with your executive director and/or medical director to discuss writing an in-depth article about the disease. Have photos, historical information, unusual facts, the name of a famous person who had the disease, etc., available for the reporter.

Identify a patient with the disease who is willing to tell his or her story. Offer a local television medical reporter the opportunity to spend part of a day with that person to better understand the challenges of living with the disease on a daily basis.

Try to book appearances with a patient and staff person on all radio public affairs programs and local television talk shows. Remember, however, that you aren't going to get to appear on these programs just because you are a nonprofit organization representing a good cause. You must have a story or hook—a compelling reason for the viewer or listener to tune in and hear your information.

Ask the religion editor at the newspaper to do a story about how faith has provided strength for a patient or how the disease has tested someone's strength.

If there is a month dedicated to the disease (like Breast Cancer Awareness Month), see if local electronic media will include a daily fact about the disease at the end of each newscast.

Ask a local reporter to be screened for the disease and report on that procedure and what it was like, on a personal level. What preparation, if any, is necessary before the test? Was it easy?

Direct Mail

Contact a local utility company to see if it will put a fact sheet on the disease in the envelope with monthly bills.

If the disease affects one age group more than others (e.g., teens, seniors), obtain mailing lists for people in that age group and mail information announcing screenings for the disease.

Speakers

Send speakers to churches' Wednesday night suppers or Thursday night prayer meetings—if they have a program, they are always looking for speakers. If appropriate, send speakers to high school assemblies. Try to get speakers scheduled at professional business group meetings to discuss the urgent need for research funding. Remember to have an interesting and unique speech model.

Special Events

Ask a corporation that partners with your agency to sponsor a screening day or week. Offer some incentive for everyone who gets screened—discount tickets to a local museum or amusement park, free French fries at a fast food restaurant, discount on eyeglasses, etc. Track the number of people who participate in this special promotion.

Have a presence at career days in local schools to encourage children to become researchers, using the disease as an example of research efforts.

Work with the fundraising staff to have children drop pennies into a giant jar at a shopping mall and then have a contest to see who can guess the amount (this can be a little staff-intensive because all the pennies have to be either rolled by hand or taken to a machine to process them before they can be deposited in the bank!). See if a local bank will sponsor this event.

Advertising

Work with a corporate partner to purchase a billboard or newspaper ad that shows the face of the disease in a creative and unforgettable way.

Determine if the local advertising club creates any *pro bono* campaigns. Or locate an advertising agency that will assist free of charge on a per-project basis.

Ask members of the board of directors to dedicate one of their business ads to the cause.

Resources
  Budgets

Working with existing program budgets, allocate funds to specific areas such as advertising or direct mail. As the plan is put into action, it will help focus on how budgets need to be built to include PR efforts. In some cases parts of the plan may not be practical because of lack of funds. If that is the case, can the board of directors or fundraising staff increase their goals to fund public relations programs for the next fiscal year?

Staff

Determine staffing for various projects. Make it clear where responsibilities lie. Too often, a small segment of the staff becomes overburdened with special events, speaking engagements, stuffing, and mailing.

Outside Help

Look at ways to accomplish goals with *pro bono* or low-cost professional assistance from PR firms, advertising agencies, interns from the communications departments of colleges and universities, and loaned executives from corporations.

Evaluation

Build measuring techniques into all of your programs. Have a simple form available to determine where people learned of the screening. See if doctors or the health department keeps records of diagnosis of the disease and compare the figures to previous years. If you do advertise, include some kind of coupon to redeem (for a soft drink or 10% off at a store) in order to measure the effectiveness of your ads. ∎

Create a plan for your organization that will accomplish what *you* want through projects that will also give the media, corporate partners, and the public something *they* want.

For corporations, the days of helping a nonprofit just because it is a good cause are pretty much gone. Business leaders today want public recognition of their good deeds and most media entities want to increase viewers, listeners, and readers because that is what they use to structure advertising rates. So, you need to craft clever win-win situations in your public relations planning. As you go through several PR plans, you will become more savvy and creative in your ideas for partnering with other organizations and for crafting sponsorships that can help you achieve your goals.

Always remember what you really want for your agency, and then use good public relations strategies to go get it. But be careful what you wish for and be prepared for things to go wrong. Had I been better prepared when the radio guys came to the science museum, I would have stopped the soundman from getting too close to the generator used in the electricity demonstration. The museum did get publicity, but it wasn't exactly the kind of exposure I had hoped to receive. Remember to expect the unexpected!

Who, What, When, Where, and Why?

▪ 3 ▪

Written communication is an essential part of any public relations program. It is not the only important element, but a vital one because what you put on paper says more about your organization than the mere words. The credibility of your agency is at stake, so it is critically important to make sure that all information presented is accurate and complete.

Part of ensuring the accuracy of an organization's written information is to put into place a policy that instructs all employees and volunteers who generate written material to route it through the staff person responsible for public relations. This will help ensure quality control for statements that reflect the agency's mission, provide a double check for dates to be sure there is no conflict with a scheduled event, and make sure all titles, phone numbers, and other important information are correct.

It is also advisable to be sensitive to agency jargon, acronyms, and repetitive phrases. One corporation sent a memo to staff announcing that the word "efficiency" was to become an integral part of the company's message about its service to customers. I read a two-page press release from this corporation in which "efficiency" was used at least ten times. The word lost its meaning by being too repetitive. After a while, instead of reading the information, I was counting how many times that word was used. Careful proofreading might have avoided that overkill.

Proofreading should be a daily part of your job. Look at the following sentence: "The pubic is invited to a moral break for parents." This was part of a press release for an organization that supported families of children with a devastating disease. A *morale* break to help lift parents' spirits was scheduled, to which the *public* was invited. Again, careful proofreading would have caught this error before it became one of the "world's funniest typos."

Don't rely solely on yourself for proofreading. It is too easy to read what you think you wrote instead of what is actually on the page. Also, while a piece may make perfect sense to you because you know all of the background, it may not communicate the same thing to the general public. Have several people proofread for typos, readability, and correctness of information. You will find people you trust to proofread for you—after you weed out those who want to edit or rewrite the entire piece. There are courses and seminars on proofreading that teach you to read a piece backwards (so you focus on every word) and other "tricks of the trade."

And please don't rely on spell check. An item a reporter wrote in the paper contained the name of the PR firm Fleishman Hillard. Someone at the paper (using spell check) changed the name to "Foilsman Halyard." The PR firm called and complained that the reporter was making fun of them.

Basically, just use common sense:

- Do dial phone numbers you are not familiar with to be sure they are correct.
- Do double-check the spelling of a difficult name.
- Don't forget to proof headlines.
- Don't rely too heavily on the spell check function on your computer. If you aren't sure about a word, look it up in your computer dictionary or go to the good old-fashioned dictionary I know you keep handy.

When reviewing written material, your accuracy check should also eliminate agency jargon and acronyms from all information that will be distributed to the general public. I once served on the publicity committee for a state CASA organization. A press release was faxed to me for comment. It was well written, typed, double-spaced, with no misspellings. It detailed the important work of the agency very well. However, nowhere in the release was it explained what CASA (Court-Appointed Special Advocates) represents.

Be careful that you do not fall into writing for the public in the same way that you communicate with coworkers.

- If your organization offers support groups led by *facilitators*, remember that many people don't know what a facilitator is—use the term "group leader" instead.
- If your agency provides services for people with a disease, don't write, "Clients receive their *meds* at our clinic." Use the word "medication" or "drug therapy" instead.
- If you work for a performing arts group, avoid writing "XYZ

Theater will *strike the set* of its current play on Tuesday." Some people have no clue what "strike" means in this context. Use "disassemble" or "take down" instead.
- And if your art gallery plans to *mount an exhibition* next month, remember that horse enthusiasts will "mount" their steed while dog breeders use the word "mount" in a totally different way!

The look of your written material is also important. What you send to the media and to the general public must look professional. Use plenty of margins—top, bottom, and both sides. Use double-space or space-and-a-half formatting for press releases, and carefully inspect the spacing in brochures and other agency materials. (Chapter 6, Why Is the "Look" Important?, will address this "look" of materials in more depth.)

There are some interesting psychological facts about printed material. For example, there is a reason most books are printed with black ink on white paper: it is easy to read. Also remember "white space is my friend." The size of your font (or typeface) is equally important. Don't be tempted to use a nine-point font to make something fit on one page. You won't be fooling anyone, just making your information harder to read. If it absolutely has to fit on one page, edit the copy to eliminate unnecessary words. Think about information you have received that is typed single-spaced, margin-to-margin. Just looking at it is intimidating because it looks like too much information to read and digest. That is why you need to have wide margins and lots of friendly white space. It makes the information you want to communicate more digestible.

Clever use of bolding, italics, and the font size on your computer can also enhance your press materials. Consider the following:

> ■ The look of your written material is also important. What you send to the media and to the general public must look professional.

Media Advisory
For More Information Contact:
Mary Smith, 111-555-0000
    Local Church Group Plans Walk-A-Thon
    Annual Walk Will Benefit Needy Families

Try this instead:

MEDIA ADVISORY
For More Information Contact:
Mary Smith, 111-555-0000
    Local Church Group Plans Walk-A-Thon
    Annual Walk Will Benefit Needy Families

This gives your media advisory immediate interest and sets it apart from the rest. Continue the release in a readable font, like Arial or Times New Roman, in 11- or 12-point size. Try this technique and see if you can measure the results in terms of interest and media coverage.

Now I get to indulge in one of my pet peeves: nonprofit organizations and the use of colored paper and the copy machine. Many organizations—not just small ones—feel compelled to make copies of flyers, announcements, fact sheets, and conference materials on colored paper. Goldenrod particularly makes me see red. Try getting out of that box and think about how to communicate effectively in new ways. Use the computer, with its variety of styles and typefaces, to create an interesting flyer. Then, if you are making more than two hundred copies, go to a quick print shop and have them make your copies. It's usually cheaper than running your beleaguered copy machine, and sometimes a printer can use a different color ink to create an interesting piece. They may give you some heavier or coated paper that was left over from another job, or let you purchase it at a bargain price. Use your imagination and think about information you receive and what you find interesting and readable. Keep a file of examples of unique materials and clever press releases and brochures for future reference.

The look of your information is important, but it won't make up for sloppy writing that contains inaccurate information. Good writing is essential. You don't have to be a prize-winning novelist to prepare a good press release. Using proper English, writing in complete sentences, and organizing your material in a logical format will do the job. There are many courses out there to teach people how to write press releases. If you are insecure about that aspect of your role as a public relations staff person or volunteer, it might not be a bad idea to look into a short course. Or, with a few tips, you might find that practice is all you need.

The length of a press release or advisory or fact sheet is debatable. Remember that all public relations professionals are not going to agree on all issues. This is one of them. Some will tell you that a hard and fast rule is to keep a release to one page and single space it. Others will say, No, two pages and double space. I personally believe that two pages is fine and that single spacing makes it hard for media representatives to read the release and edit it for their use.

I would never have suggested that a press release be, oh, fourteen pages long! I was horrified when an employee presented me with a "Six-Month Press Release" that was, in fact, fourteen pages long. "No one will ever read this," I shrieked. "Trust me," she said. Following the belief that one should never say never, I allowed her to send the release out. It

> Keep a file of unique, clever press releases and brochures for future reference.

listed all of the upcoming events for the next six months. It provided general facts about the organization and listed ongoing and permanent events and activities. That was three years ago. Today, the media contact that organization if the six-month press release is late.

I learned a valuable lesson: When you work with a nonprofit (like a cultural attraction or an educational facility) that has permanent activities and other events that are in place for a limited time, media calendar editors and news assignment editors can use the more detailed information for their planning purposes. A longer press release may also work for:

- Agencies that offer instruction to the public—such as classes on how to deal with your teenager or workshops on retirement planning
- A humane society that offers periodic off-site adoptions

For most releases, however, like an announcement of new board of directors' members or a call for volunteers to stuff envelopes, keep your information to two pages or less and use adequate spacing.

When writing a press release, it's important to put a contact name, title, and telephone number at the top of the page, along with when the information is to be released, i.e., "For Immediate Release" or "For Release After Noon on October 22, 2002." Also remember Who, What, When, Where, and Why. The five Ws are good friends to have when trying to communicate information about an event or activity your organization is promoting. The five Ws help you remember not to leave out anything crucial—like when and where the 10K race starts! Include them in the lead paragraph, both to get a reporter's attention and to provide all of the information needed in case the release is edited. The lead (first paragraph) of the release needs to be short and simple.

> The Similar Syndromes Foundation (S.S.F.) [WHO] announces a new screening test [WHAT] that will provide medical documentation for people finding it difficult to get a diagnosis for Similar Syndromes. This new program will give patients positive proof of their disease, which will pave the way for insurance and government benefits [WHY]. All county health departments [WHERE] will have this free test available by the end of March [WHEN].

Most public relations practitioners use an inverted pyramid style for press releases, in which you present the most important and interesting information first. After the lead paragraph, include a slightly longer paragraph to explain the hows and whys. Follow with a third paragraph containing more details, quotes from relevant people, and any other interesting information about the event or organization. See page 21 for a sample press release.

Beyond press releases, your agency's written communication may include community calendar notices, which can basically be an expanded lead paragraph from your press release. For a calendar notice, be sure to use the five Ws to ensure that you include all pertinent information. The calendar notice is sent to media representatives at newspapers and radio and television stations who handle the organizing and posting of events taking place in your geographical area. Calendar listings are an important resource for people trying to decide what activity to do for the weekend: seniors looking for gardening classes, weekend jocks wanting to participate in a bike ride or competitive walk or run, or parents looking for family events. Most print media organizations include calendars, although some (like business magazines) will target their specific audience. It's just common sense that you don't send a notice about a diaper derby to a golf magazine! Review the material in Chapter 4, Why Must I Have Media Relations?, for more details on the importance of (and how to get to know) the media and their audience.

Another often-overlooked written communication resource is the letter to the editor. This is an effective tool when used correctly. Consider the letter to the editor as:

- A short reply (under two hundred words) to an issue in the news
- A nonjudgmental correction to an oversight a reporter may have made in a story
- A thank-you to a volunteer or donor
- A way of expanding upon a news story

There was a wonderful article in the local newspaper about the future of electric vehicles. The story, taken from a wire service, was interesting and fairly comprehensive, even though it reported on an activity in another state. The local paper neglected to mention, however, that there was an important electric vehicle research center right in the same town. A letter to the editor from the research center's board president and executive director was quickly faxed to the newspaper saying how much more interesting that story might have been for readers if the local connection had been included. The letter was printed in the newspaper and a follow-up local story was later written.

Your agency's annual report is another important communication tool that should utilize the five Ws. (This type of document will be discussed in detail in Chapter 7, What Publications Do I Need?) Agency brochures, fundraising pieces—most material you or someone in your

> Calendar listings are an important resource for people trying to decide what activity to do for the weekend.

■

PRESS RELEASE

For Immediate Release   **Phone: 111-222-3333**
Similar Syndromes Foundation   **Fax: 111-222-3333**

New screening test available for diagnosis of Similar Syndromes

The Similar Syndromes Foundation (S.S.F.) announces a new screening test that will provide medical documentation for people finding it difficult to get a diagnosis for Similar Syndromes. This new program will give patients positive proof of their disease, which will pave the way for insurance and government benefits. All county health departments will have this free test available by the end of March.

This kind of screening test has been in the research labs for several years, but only recently was the procedure refined so that it is inexpensive, fast, and reliable for all patients. The test, called Alpha 5one2, can detect Similar Syndromes (a random disease of fluctuating symptoms involving the immune system) in its earliest stages. Researchers at the Smithfield Center in Anytown were elated that their work has finally reached the point where Alpha 5one2 can be used on a routine basis.

Dr. John Doe, director of the research project, said, "This is indeed a breakthrough. We have watched helplessly for far too long as S.S. patients suffered for years before a definitive test could give them the documentation they needed for financial help."

Most S.S. patients do not qualify for government benefits until solid documentation of their disease is available. This test will provide them with that earlier option.

For more information on Alpha 5one2 or to locate a health department in a specific area, call 111-222-3333 or visit the S.S.F. website at (your website here).

**Address Here • (111) 222-3333 FAX (111) 222-3333
website here • E-mail address**

agency writes—should pass the five-W test in order to communicate as effectively as possible.

As the public relations representative for your nonprofit, you are responsible for letting your constituents, donor sources, and the general public know as many of the Whos, Whats, Whens, Wheres, and Whys of your agency as you can. The written word is one excellent way to do that. But remember to include all five Ws. If you just communicate Who, Why, and When, your audience will be clueless about What and Where. The result will be detrimental to the activity or event you want to promote, and it will create negative feelings about your organization. So, remember the five Ws. They may even bring you to new insights about your organization. For example, in trying to explain why you are doing something, you might just realize that you should be doing something else instead.

Why Must I Have Media Relations?

· 4 ·

Media relations is one of the most difficult elements of a public relations practitioner's job. It's an intricate dance in which all the elements must be carefully choreographed.

Former Miss America Marilyn Van Derbur spoke at an annual state conference just months after she had revealed that her wealthy father had sexually abused her for years. Now here was a big story. Advisories were sent to the local media, offering the opportunity to interview the celebrity. Three television stations and one radio station actually called to say they would cover the event and wanted to interview her.

The morning of the event, confirmation phone calls were made to the stations to be sure all the information they needed would be available. In a perfect example of how capricious the media can be, one reporter apologized profusely because her assignment editor had pulled her from the Miss America story to cover the pollen count, which was higher than it had ever been in the city. In fact, all three stations made the judgment that more of their viewers suffer from pollen-related allergies than were affected by child sexual abuse. So, while TV camera crews were shooting video of pollen-covered cars and people sneezing, there were no media present when Marilyn Van Derbur uttered one of the best "sound bites" I have ever heard: "Like red dye dropped into a can of white paint, the abuse colored every aspect of my life."

This example illustrates two important elements of media relations. One is that using celebrities to get publicity for your cause is often very effective. The second is that sometimes the draw of the celebrity is overruled by the local media's determination of what viewers, readers, and listeners in their coverage area want to know. In this case, the media powers that be decided to go with the pollen.

When something like that happens, one of the most difficult things to accomplish as a public relations staffer is to convince your boss or board chair that you really can't make the media do anything. You can encourage them, you can even get a commitment from them, but you can never guarantee coverage.

Creating a Media Guide

For a nonprofit to use media effectively for public awareness benefits, there are some essential steps to take. The first, and one of the most important, is to create a media guide—a comprehensive listing of all the media organizations you will need to contact, whether local, regional, national, or international.

The public relations firm Cohn & Wolfe publishes a local media guide each year in Atlanta and Chicago. For a nominal fee, organizations can order the guide, which contains listings for daily and weekly newspapers, periodicals, broadcast bureaus, statewide media associations, news and broadcast services, and television and radio stations. There are also national services that provide publication directories, but they can be very expensive. Check with public relations firms in your area to find out if any of them provide this kind of valuable service. Look on the Internet to see if your state's press association publishes media contact information for the entire state, or go directly to a specific media entity by searching on the web using the name of the newspaper or radio station as the keyword. Ask if members of your board of directors can share media lists from their companies' public relations department.

If a preprinted or borrowed media guide is not available in your area, create your own. It isn't difficult, just labor-intensive. List daily and weekly newspapers, neighborhood newsletters, magazines, online information outlets, and television and radio stations. This can be done on the computer, with a hard copy kept in a loose-leaf notebook for easy reference and updating. Creating the guide will involve major telephone and/or computer work in the beginning. Call each media outlet (or go to its website) and find out the correct mailing address, fax number, e-mail address, names of pertinent editors, and other information that will make contacting that media organization more efficient and effective. Volunteers or interns can be helpful in gathering the information you need.

> You really can't make the media do anything. You can encourage them, you can even get a commitment from them, but you can never guarantee coverage.

A sample listing might look like this:

```
WXYZ-TV, Channel 2              (555) 555-5555 - Main switchboard
CBS Affiliate Station           (555) 555-1234 - Newsroom
    25 Elm Street               e-mail - wxyztv@mindspring.com
    Anywhere, USA 33333         (555) 555- 3434 - Fax

    Vice President/General Manager        John Smith
    News Director                         Ed Johnson
    Public Service/Public Affairs         Susan Cute
    News Assignment Editor - days         Mary Jones
    News Assignment Editor - weekends     Sam White
    Newscasts       7:00 a.m. Anchors     Jim Knot and Jane Doe
                    Noon Anchors          Jane Doe and Kyle Terry
                    6:00 p.m. Anchors     Kyle Terry and Jim Knot

    Locally Produced Show "Inside Anywhere"     Producer - Jim Knot
```

This gives you a quick reference for this station. You can add any pertinent notes, such as, "Jane Doe does not make appearances on Sundays because of religious commitments." Or "Do not call news department one hour prior to scheduled broadcasts." Note the music format for radio stations. A rock station may not be appropriate for your needs, while a country music station might be just right. You should also include information on which reporters or editors prefer faxes, e-mail, or telephone contact.

For print media, it is helpful to list editors for the various sections of the paper, such as business editor or food editor. Based on the nature of your organization, you will develop more frequent relationships with some media representatives, such as the health reporter or the theater critic. Also, when listing newspapers and periodicals, ask for their most current circulation figures. These can be helpful when trying to evaluate the effectiveness of your public relations efforts. And remember, three things are considered givens with media personnel:

1. They change jobs a lot.
2. They hate to have their names misspelled.
3. They really hate to receive mail addressed to their predecessors.

Be sure to keep your media guide updated. Updating your media

■ Be sure to keep your media guide updated.

guide every three months is good, but also be alert to changes you see announced—like a newscast's format change or new personnel at the newspaper or radio station. Check your newspaper to see if it carries a weekly column on radio, television, or in magazines.

After your media guide is complete, it is time to get to know media representatives in your area. I can't stress strongly enough how important it is to read newspapers and local magazines, watch local newscasts, and listen to radio stations. I always monitor local programs. I listen to different radio stations wherever I am driving in my car. There is a tiny TV on my desk to keep track of local programs, like *Good Morning, Anywhere USA,* and news shows. If there is a press club in your town or city, join it as a public relations professional. Most press clubs will allow public relations people to join for a higher fee than is charged the working media. Attending press club events is a good way to meet media representatives. Better still, volunteer to work on a press club committee. Network and pay attention to what is happening in your town's media community. Getting to know who's who and what's what at your media outlets will give you another way to stay just a little ahead of all those other organizations bombarding the media.

Press Kits

Another step in preparation for working with the media is to have appropriate materials ready when there is a request for information. You should construct a general press kit and have it available so that other staff can send it out when requests come in during your absence. Use a presentation folder with pockets to bring together a packet of material that will provide information about your organization for a reporter to keep on file and use. The press kit should include:

- A brief history of your organization
- A description of services provided
- A page of your agency logo in camera-ready form with the logo represented in several sizes
- A general press release
- Your logo and images on a CD
- Complete contact information: name, title, address, phone, e-mail, fax, and cell phone

Note that you should also have your logo and visual images in an online version that can be transmitted electronically or downloaded by the media. Obtain good quality photos/images that show some kind of action. Use tight or close-in shots and identify everyone in the picture. Have multiple copies made in black-and-white, glossy format and in

> Getting to know who's who and what's what at your media outlets will give you another way to stay just a little ahead of all those other organizations bombarding the media.

color. Most periodicals prefer color and many newspapers are using more color. You can use 3- by 5-inch prints and color slides or transparencies. Have your photographer take the same or similar shots in these formats. Investigate having photos and your logo available on compact disk. This is rapidly becoming the preferred format for most media organizations and for printers.

Beyond the general agency press kit, tailor material for specific events. Your annual conference will have its own press information packet, for example.

You should also have video available—often called "B roll" by the media. Try to persuade a video production company to shoot some generic B roll of your agency's activities and have copies available on beta tape (which television stations prefer) as well as on VHS tape for showing on VCRs at meetings or during potential donor presentations. Having these materials readily available will increase your chances of getting media coverage because visuals add interest to a story.

Timing is Everything

When do you contact the media? When you first assume public relations duties, send a press kit to key media personnel with a note introducing yourself as the PR contact at your agency. After that, it really depends on what you and your nonprofit organization are doing. If you contact the news department, make sure the news you offer is genuine or that the idea you pitch fits with the format of the station. Pitch your idea based on its importance to the public interest instead of its importance to your agency. Learn to think from the media's side of the fence.

I called a children's reporter once to propose an idea about the science museum being an excellent resource for families to help their children decide on what to do for the "dreaded science project." It so happened that her nine-year-old daughter was going through that very agony. The reporter understood firsthand why viewers would be interested in the story and was able to convince her producer to use it. The museum got a beautiful feature story on the evening news. (And the reporter's daughter got an A on her science project!) Timing is everything! But I also knew this reporter and understood that she would listen to my rationale about this story idea because she did have a child in school. Research about the reporters and editors in your local media is so important.

Obviously, if you have genuine news, you should contact the media. When the remains of six servicemen were returned from South Vietnam fifteen years after the war, I contacted local media to offer interviews

> Pitch your idea based on its importance to the public interest instead of its importance to your agency. Learn to think from the media's side of the fence.

with local families of men still listed as Prisoner of War or Missing in Action in Southeast Asia. The families had agreed to be interviewed ahead of time. The media appreciated the opportunity to give a local slant to the story. If your agency works with AIDS patients and a new drug treatment for AIDS is announced, contact the media to interview local people who might be impacted by the announcement.

Anytime you can provide the media with a way to localize a national or regional news story, they will be appreciative because it helps them do their job—which is to interest local readers, listeners, or viewers, so they will buy papers, watch TV, and listen to radio programs. That's how the stations can keep advertising rates at a profitable level. In anticipation of the need for localization, prepare a list of people ahead of time who are willing to be interviewed, for example (depending on your organization): people who have been through your parenting classes, cancer survivors or people currently in treatment, volunteers who deliver meals to the elderly, or people living with a disability.

If your organization has a program in place that addresses a need discussed in the news, call a local reporter. A statewide organization offers a specific after-school program where children and adolescents can participate in organized, supervised activities. In the news, Jane Fonda (who works for prevention of teen pregnancy) announces plans to work with kids after school. That's when many teenage girls become pregnant because they are at home alone for two hours after school while both parents work. Ah-ha! This is a perfect time to let local reporters know that such an after-school project is already in existence in the community and could be expanded with additional volunteers and funding.

- Your nonprofit is holding a chili cookout as a fundraiser—send information to the food editor.
- Your museum is doing an exhibition on Albert Einstein, who, besides being a Nobel Prize–winning physicist, also helped establish the Jewish homeland. Pitch the religion editor for a story on whether or not science and a belief in God can coexist.
- Your organization partners with a commercial sponsor to move into new office space—contact the business editor.
- Your youth volunteers plant and maintain vegetable gardens for senior citizens—the garden editor might be interested.

Well, you get the picture. . . . Hopefully you'll get a picture and a good story!

How to Contact the Media

The next question is how do you contact the media? The answer depends, in part, upon the media. Many media representatives simply don't like faxed press releases, and I suspect you won't either because it is almost impossible to get a fax through to a TV or radio station when you are in your office. A fax service may be the answer. This is a business that charges you a small fee (usually with special rates for nonprofits) to put information in a daily fax that is sent to media outlets and public relations and marketing firms each morning. This is an excellent way to be sure you reach the news assignment editor first thing when plans are being made for what will be covered that day. This kind of service is ideal on the day of an event to encourage coverage. It is best used in support of a media advisory that was mailed a couple of weeks prior to the event. A quick phone call to see if the assignment editor plans to have someone cover your event, or to determine if additional information or materials are needed, may also help. It is imperative, however, that you stay sensitive to which media in your area want to be called and are responsive to follow-up calls and which really don't want to be called.

Many newspapers now include reporters' e-mail addresses with their stories. It does seem to work well to e-mail a pitch to editors or reporters. If they are interested, they will call you for details, but if they simply can't use your idea, they can quickly e-mail you back and be done with it—no irritating telephone tag. I don't think e-mailing a press release is a good idea, however, and *never* send unsolicited e-mail attachments of any kind. You can certainly include an e-mail address in the contact information.

For now, good old "snail mail" is still a good bet as your staple communication with the media, although this is changing rapidly, especially in larger media markets. For now, use faxes and e-mail wisely to supplement hard copies of press releases and community calendar information. But do start asking if some reporters or editors prefer electronic communication instead of regular mail. Technology is changing so fast that electronic communication may soon become the norm. Note in your media guide who will take faxes and e-mail. Become proficient in attaching documents to e-mail (only if requested) and copying files to disk for those media reps who prefer to work that way. Install a good anti-virus program on your computer so you don't unwittingly either send or accept infected files. If you have a web page—and you should— be sure to include that address in all the material you send to the media. That makes it easy for them to check out your organization and may

It is imperative that you stay sensitive to which media in your area want and are responsive to follow-up calls and which really don't want to be called.

Note in your media guide who will take faxes and e-mail.

spark their imagination for a story idea you never thought about.

However you contact the media, think carefully about how you follow up. As you work with them, you will start to know which editors appreciate a phone call to make sure they received your information and which ones really hate those calls. Schedule your calls in the morning before any strategy meetings where reporters discuss the day and are given assignments. Never call a television newsroom just prior to or when the news is on the air. When you do call, keep it short; simply determine that they received your information and ask if they need more information. Never beg ("This is really important and my boss says I have to get coverage . . .") or threaten ("My brother knows your general manager and he can talk to him . . ."). Don't be a pest; just be professional and understand that if you are calling, there are probably many others calling as well.

The subject of follow-up calls is tricky. Older PR practitioners and some public relations firms swear by them. In simpler times, a quick phone call from a PR person to make sure the press release was received may have worked. Today, media staff are bombarded with calls. A PR firm may feel the need to make calls as a way to reassure a client that they are doing all they can to place a story. But don't overdo the phone calling. I worked for one editor who, after four phone messages from a PR person "checking" on the story, decided that if the woman called one more time, she would not publish the story no matter how good it was. That's the kind of information you need to find out. Best bet—don't try to follow up on a standard press release. Unless you have something out of the ordinary, rethink calling.

Thank You

Be sure to say thank you when you do receive coverage. Send a letter to the reporter with copies to the show's producer, news director, and general manager. Express your organization's gratitude for covering the event and then provide information on how the coverage helped—"A total of 120 people gave blood because of your outstanding coverage" or "Thirty-five people were screened for sickle-cell anemia." This gives radio and television stations letters for their license-renewal file and newspapers can use the "thank-you" as a letter to the editor to demonstrate their own community spirit. Besides that, all human beings like to be thanked for a job well done. If there were "slight" mistakes in the story—and we all make them—don't try to correct them unless the error was something really bad, like reporting that you have found a cure for the disease when you were only announcing a new treatment.

You Are the Expert—Become a Resource for the Media

As you continue to work with the media, establish yourself as the person to contact for your agency's expert information. This system works well as a win-win situation for both your organization and the media. If you are with a zoo, let the media know that if someone's pet monkey gets loose in a neighborhood, your staff can be interviewed about the typical behavior of monkeys and what people should do if they encounter the wayward primate. If you work for a church day care center and have a director with a master's degree in early childhood education, make it known that the director is available for interviews about how to deal with a child's temper tantrum in the grocery store. Your goal is to become a card in the reporter's Rolodex—a reliable resource for that reporter. Also remember that if you can't provide the information the reporter needs, try to refer him or her to someone who can get the information. That reporter is on deadline and will remember that you were helpful in getting him or her to a good source for information.

> Your goal is to become a card in the reporter's Rolodex—a reliable resource for that reporter.

What Happened to PSAs?

Years ago, television stations routinely ran a generous number of public service announcements (PSAs) for nonprofit organizations. That is no longer the case. The Federal Communications Commission (FCC) deregulated—did away with—the requirement that radio and TV stations include a set number of public service spot announcements in their weekly program logs as a condition of their broadcast license. Stations now do community awareness activities because they want to be good citizens—not because their license renewal depends on it. For that reason, the nature of PSAs has changed. With this deregulation of radio and TV stations' obligation, is there really such a thing as a PSA anymore? Well, yes and no. The term is still used to define the free support stations give to nonprofits, but the days are long gone when you could expect stations in most major markets to produce a thirty-second spot for organizations. It may still happen in some smaller markets and networks that use public service spots produced by the national Ad Council, but, for the most part, PSAs have become shared IDs (the nonprofit's logo and station logo on a slide that is aired at the top of the hour), community calendar announcements, appearances on public affairs programs, and brief mentions on the news.

When I worked as public service director of a CBS-affiliate TV station in the early 1970s, I had my own film crew and went on location to film, and later videotape, PSAs. I was able to schedule studio time to produce my own spots (although the crew got very unhappy when I did a spot with puppies and babies, all of whom felt nature's call during production of the spot). I had one hundred 30- and 60-second spots a month to fill with PSAs from nonprofit organizations. Alas, those days are no more, so nonprofits have to be creative in order to garner airtime.

Today, there are even more agencies doing good work, but there are far fewer opportunities for free airtime, which is one reason to be creative and think "out of the box" for publicity. Create your own PSAs:

- During Women's History Month, offer the local TV station two or three lines about outstanding women in the state to use during the newscast each weekday evening.
- Invite the news anchor to be the master of ceremonies at your agency's black tie gala.
- Offer the station's weather department the opportunity to place a remote weather station in your facility.

Think, think, think!

> The bottom line for the media is what will make people watch, listen, or read.

What Do Media Organizations Want?

You need to understand that the bottom line for the media is what will make people watch, listen, or read. The more people the station or newspaper can document, the more they can charge for advertising. The more they can charge for advertising, the more money they make and the happier they are. So, when you want to have the media do something for your agency (whether it is to promote an upcoming event or cover a major announcement about research), try to keep their bottom line in mind and structure your request so it will help that media entity attract viewers, listeners, or subscribers. Covering a speech by a local Boy Scout leader to the Kiwanis club probably isn't going to get much coverage because it is not visually interesting and there won't be any young scouts at the meeting. The Cub Scout Pinewood Derby, however, is a natural for media coverage because it is exciting, with good audio and visuals when all those little boys race their homemade cars. It is also appealing to the media because so many people in the community either were Cub Scouts, are den leaders, have children who are Scouts, or have toddlers who will be Scouts.

Make it Easy for the Media

You are competing with so many other good causes. In a major city, there could be five hundred to one thousand or more registered nonprofits. The easier you make it for the media to cover your event, the better your chances. Here are some tips:

- Have your general press kit available. (See page 26 for details on how to create a press kit.)

- Have an electronic press kit available with the same material that is in the paper version. Include your logo and images that can be downloaded.
- Tailor the press kit for each specific event with pertinent information and contacts.
- If you are asking for coverage, provide a person who can escort the media representative to make sure power is available if needed, have an agency official nearby to appear on camera or in a photo, be sure good visual possibilities are pointed out, and make sure access is provided to activities and personalities pertinent to the story.

Press Conferences

And finally, do you think anyone comes to press conferences anymore? Back in the "good old days," all you had to do was have food available and the media would show up. Today, there are too many press conferences and too few of them really need to be called at all. Don't call a press conference to announce that your organization has a new board chair—unless that person is a former president of the United States or a popular professional basketball player. Do call a press conference if Princess Caroline of Monaco has agreed to support your organization and will be in town to appear at a benefit.

I called a press conference once for coverage of a "major announcement" by the board of directors of a child-serving organization and a woman whose baby had apparently been abducted. This woman had become a media favorite during the weeks following the tragedy. When the baby was discovered dead in a shallow grave, apparently killed by the father, this young woman decided to donate to my organization the funds that had been raised to find the child. It was a very successful press conference and a touching moment that called attention to the services my agency provided and to the heartache of families touched by violence. However, these kinds of opportunities are rare.

Instead of the traditional press conference, try a media day. Have agency staff and volunteers in a central location for a designated period of time to talk to any media personnel who wish to come by. Be sure to have articulate spokespeople and good visuals. For the Similar Syndromes Foundation, when the Alpha 5one2 screening test is made public, the media is invited to view an exhibit with photographs showing the scientists at work and colorful diagrams of how the test can diagnose the ailment. Have medical doctors available for comment and provide solid statistics on how much money people will save in medical procedures by being diagnosed early.

Try holding an online press conference if your agency has the technology to do so. Media personnel can log on from their desks for a press conference with the mayor or police chief or a celebrity visiting town to promote a new movie. There are numerous ways to format an event like this—investigate what works best for your agency.

Bottom Line

Media relations can be fun—if you figure out how all the pieces of the puzzle fit and you understand that you are really never in control. Always remember that the media don't owe you anything. Use good common sense coupled with information you are able to gather about the "personality" of the media in your town. Each town, city, and region has a distinct media personality. Mostly, media relations comes down to hard work, good research, creative thinking, timing, and luck.

> Media relations comes down to hard work, good research, creative thinking, timing, and luck.

INTERVIEW WITH A REPORTER

Jeffry Scott, staff writer for the *Atlanta Journal-Constitution*, a large daily newspaper, agreed to let the tables be turned and be the one answering the questions instead of asking them. Here is his advice to people in nonprofit organizations seeking newspaper coverage:

You must have a story angle and a really good reason that the newspaper should run the story. There need to be pros and cons and even some dramatic tension. Think about what you want to read in a newspaper. If what you are pitching isn't something you personally would want to read, don't pitch the story.

Let's take Save the Snails as an example. Why should I care about snails? Tell me that they are important to the environment and are on the brink of extinction because so many people in France are eating them! Give me access to a snail herder who is losing snails to poachers who are snatching snails for restaurants.

Or, I can give you a great example. The *New York Times* did a story on people in the South eating dirt. I read it! If it had just been a story about the dirt I wouldn't have cared, but I really wanted to find out why people would actually *eat* dirt.

Try to develop a feel for niche marketing. Know where your organization fits in at the newspaper. Research what a specific reporter does— what kind of stories does he write? Then go to the right person with a pithy story pitch. Not only will you save everybody's time, you will also flatter the reporter by letting him know you actually read what he writes and associate his name with his stories. It really is important to get to know individual reporters because they are all different.

I asked Jeffry to describe the worst thing a public relations person had ever done while he was at the newspaper.

"Here is one cardinal rule: Never send one of those naked dancer grams or marching band things to the newsroom. I've seen that happen three or four times here. And it always makes the writer and editors want to strangle the PR person. And the story doesn't get written. A cute pitch is a dead end in this business because it comes off as the last resort of a scoundrel PR type."

Here are some do's and don'ts that Jeffry suggests you memorize:

- Keep your story pitch to one page—preferably one paragraph—and write it like a breaking news story with a great lead sentence, like "National organization warns snails may soon disappear from the face of the earth!"
- Know your newspaper and where your organization fits in, then have an angle for your story that compels people to read it.
- Provide access for the reporter to interview someone other than the chairman of the board or executive director. If you are an agency helping families, let the reporter talk to a family that has benefited from your program.
- Don't engage in shameless aggrandizing or overplay something. If you say your program is the first of its kind or the biggest, make sure that is correct.
- E-mail is a good way to contact a reporter. In your e-mail say that you will follow up with a phone call.
- When you do call a reporter, always ask if he is on deadline and if he says he is, don't keep talking. Ask when would be a better time to call back.
- Don't fax information unless you are requested to do so. Faxes often get lost or tossed. Reporters don't usually check their fax boxes unless they are expecting something.

And finally, Jeffry has this to say: "There is a difference between being persistent and hounding someone. The worst mistake PR people can make is not to let go. The people who won't take no for an answer or won't listen to you when you say no are very aggravating. If a reporter says no, don't take it personally. Say thanks and get back to them at another time with a better angle." ■

I appreciate Jeffry's taking the time to share his opinions. He echoes what many reporters have said and brings up the central issue for all media: You must have a good story and an appropriate angle to get coverage for your organization beyond the calendar listings. The best way for you to understand what the various media organizations in your town want is to get to know them. If you have the opportunity to sit down over a cup of coffee with a reporter from your local newspaper, it is well worth the time spent because it will save time and frustration (on both sides) later.

When Is Something "Off the Record"?

· 5 ·

When is something "off the record"? The answer to that question is easy—never! That's why media training for your organization's key staff and volunteers is so vital. Whether the training is done by a professional or provided by you, media training can help your agency avoid future problems.

Some years ago, I insisted on media training for all staff in my organization after a particular interview that went wrong. "Mary" was a lovely, gentle Southern woman who worked in a parenting program. She was highly educated, experienced, and well respected in her field. During an interview for a newspaper, she told the reporter that parents should never spank a child under the age of three. Moments later she added, "And, off the record, I think everyone should own a pet before they have children, because the way you treat an animal is indicative of how you will treat your kids."

When the article was printed, the headline read: "Parenting Expert Says People Should Be Required to Have Pets Before They Have Kids." In the story, her comment about never spanking a child under the age of three was reported correctly, but an assumption was then made that it is all right to spank older children. That was not what the parenting program taught.

None of this was the fault of the person being interviewed. She was just not aware of the ways in which a reporter can use nuances to make a story more sensational. One goal of media training is to help an agency's spokespeople be aware of some of the pitfalls associated with interviews.

There are many skilled individuals and companies that provide media training. Sometimes you can bargain to utilize those services *pro bono*, ask for a reduced nonprofit rate, or negotiate a trade-out for tickets to your venue, free attendance at classes your agency provides, or a free membership in your organization. I believe that even if you have to pay full price, professional media training is well worth the expenditure. However, the reality may be that it is too expensive for your budget. If that is the case, you can assist staff and volunteers in their preparation to appear on camera for television, or to be interviewed on radio or by a print reporter. Review the information in this chapter, then look on the Internet or in the library for more detailed discussions on media training.

Most nonprofit organizations want the opportunity to give interviews to the media for a variety of reasons. They believe the publicity will help the organization in efforts to solicit donations, find volunteers, or make sure people who can benefit from the services provided by the agency know that those services are available.

As discussed in Chapter 4, Why Must I Have Media Relations?, I also recommend that organizations work hard to establish themselves as the local "expert" in a particular field so reporters will call *them* for interviews and use the nonprofit agency as a resource.

Once you get an interview scheduled, think about the purpose of that exposure—from both your perspective and that of the newspaper reporter or TV station. Has this reporter or station covered your agency before? Are they using this interview to provide a local slant to a regional or national story? Is the reporter looking for something you can't provide?

The national office of the Cystic Fibrosis Foundation (CFF) received a request for an interview. The public relations director asked the right questions and determined that the reason for the interview was in response to an individual who had conducted a press conference in a major city, dressed in a penguin suit, touting megadoses of a mineral as a cure for cystic fibrosis. The public relations staff did not decline the interview but did make sure the CFF spokesperson stayed totally focused on available treatments for the disease and on what medical research has shown megadoses of that particular mineral can do to the human body.

The focus was on the facts, not on the absurdity of the penguin suit or the merits of the claim. If the reporter was seeking a spokesperson from CFF to criticize either the claim or the manner of obtaining publicity for the claim, he or she was disappointed. CFF maintained both its professionalism and its credibility.

Remember two important points:

- First, think carefully before declining an interview. Declining may make it appear that the agency has something to hide or is afraid to comment for some reason.

- Second, never comment on what another individual or agency does or doesn't do. It might be the goal of a reporter to have you say another organization should have done something differently. That is *not* your role.

Sometimes, reporters will ask a nonprofit for an interview in reaction to a story that may seem not at all related. A child dies at the hands of a drunken stepfather because he cannot make the child stop crying. Complaints had previously been made to the state family and children's office about this potentially dangerous situation. A reporter wants a representative from a nonprofit, child-serving, social service agency to stand in front of the house in which the child died and say that the state agency should have removed the child from the home. Wrong! The private nonprofit has no knowledge of the case except what has been reported in the news. It is not the business of one agency to comment (on or off the record) on how another agency should act.

Interviews with nonprofit agencies are not usually so brutal, but don't be lulled into thinking the media is a big, fluffy pussycat. They are, on the whole, nice people. However, they have a job to do. Remember that, respect that, and keep your radar turned on. News departments in all media organizations are under pressure from station owners to keep ratings up—that's why there are so many investigative reports, whistle-blower stories, and consumer hot lines. Television news is a fiercely competitive business and if there is a way to sensationalize a story that will draw in more viewers, a reporter will look at that angle. Always keep that in mind.

Prior to an interview:

- Learn what you can about the media organization itself. Is it a network affiliate that could provide the story for national air? What is the reporter's specialty—investigative reporting, children's issues, the arts? These kinds of things should be in your media guide (see Chapter 4, Why Must I Have Media Relations?).
- Provide the reporter with as much background information as possible about your organization, the services it provides, and the person being interviewed. Have a simple fact sheet available, along with a list of suggested questions (especially if your agency deals with something in need of explanation to the general public—like how heart attacks happen). You can get the information to the reporter by taking it by the station yourself, sending a courier, faxing it, or e-mailing it. Find out what the reporter prefers and make it as easy as possible; your assistance will be

> Don't be lulled into thinking the media is a big, fluffy pussycat.

appreciated.

- Before the interview, think of all the possible negative questions that could be asked. Then prepare for positive answers to those questions. "Isn't it true that the efforts of the Similar Syndrome Foundation have never cured one single patient?" The response: "Unfortunately, there is no cure for the Similar Syndrome condition. However, S.S.F. has been able to dramatically improve the quality of life for all patients."
- For interviews on public affairs programs on both radio and television, ask if the host would like to have a list of suggested questions to ask you or your spokesperson.

While the reporter digests everything you provided, prepare the person to be interviewed. Here are some tips that can apply to both print and broadcast interviews:

- Sit up straight. Whether on-air or simply talking to a print reporter, you look more confident and assured if your posture is good.
- For television, wear solids or muted patterns (no white shirts) and don't wear dangling earrings or necklaces. Wear a suit jacket—not a tie-dyed T-shirt. Don't wear clothes that are too tight, uncomfortable, or will be wrinkled by the time you drive from home to the interview site. Even if this is a print interview, you present a more professional air if you are dressed professionally.
- Smile. Even on radio, listeners can hear a smile in your voice.
- Speak with energy. A droning monotone sounds boring and can result in a boring interview.
- Think "sound bites." Describe your fundraiser as "having good clean fun turning the abandoned dump into a park."
- You can use notes for print and radio interviews, but it's not a good idea for television.
- Don't ramble. Make your point, but do it briefly.
- Mention your organization often. Don't say, "We provide disaster relief," but rather, "The American Red Cross provides disaster relief."

When your spokesperson is being interviewed, that individual represents the agency. Personal opinions shouldn't be voiced because they may be taken as the opinion or philosophy of the organization. Make responses to questions energetic, compelling, and better than the average interview you see on the evening news.

Remember that the reporter is not your parent, your teacher, or your boss. You really are in charge. It is okay to correct a misstatement made by the reporter. It is fine to keep the interview on track. You can say, "I don't know," or "I can't answer that question," although there are differing opinions on using the phrase "no comment" because it may convey the need to hide information. I personally believe that saying "no comment" does more harm than good. It is better to say "That is an area I cannot discuss at this time" or "I don't have all of the facts to answer that question right now, but I will be glad to provide you that information as soon as I can."

One of the most important pieces of advice I ever received was that if you are in an interview and the reporter is like a pit bull and won't let go of a question you will not or cannot answer, just look into the camera or at the reporter and *say nothing*. That works especially well if the interview is live because nothing is worse on radio or TV than "dead air." It also works with print reporters, who get nervous when the conversation stops. It takes a lot of discipline and courage on your part because you will also be uncomfortable with silence. In some cases, however, silence really is golden.

What we are talking about with interviews is communicating with words. Most people don't remember everything they said during an interview. As the person responsible for public relations, you should always be present at interviews. You are there to listen. You are also the interviewee's safety net. It is perfectly okay to stop an interview. Tell the print reporter that the interview is over if he goes places he was told were off limits. You do have rights. It may be a good idea to tape the interview to listen to it later with the person who was interviewed—in a private place with the pressure off—so you can analyze the strengths and weaknesses of the interview.

When ValuJet held its annual meeting just three weeks after a horrible crash in the Florida Everglades, a PR intern from the nonprofit facility where the meeting was being held was posted outside the meeting room. This was a precaution in case zealous media tried to get visuals of the off-limits stockholders' meeting held prior to the press conference. The room featured glass windows. There were blinds on all the windows, but a glass door was not covered. Sure enough, a big, burly cameraman from a television network decided to try to shoot video of the meeting through the glass. The intern, a rising senior in college, was stunned. Not really sure what to do but determined to perform her assigned task, she raised the paper she was holding, placed it in front of the camera lens, and yelled for the security guard. She did exactly the right thing. The cameraman was escorted away and the intern had quite a tale to tell in school in the fall!

Remember that the reporter is not your parent, your teacher, or your boss. You really are in charge.

(Note: I must add that ValuJet did one of the most amazing jobs of crisis communication I have ever witnessed following that unfortunate crash in 1996. See Chapter 12, What Do I Do in a Crisis Situation?, for more information on managing difficult situations that arise in your agency.)

So, you have been successful in scheduling an interview, the celebrity representing your agency did a fabulous job communicating all the right information, the interview has aired or been printed. Your job is over, right? Not quite. It is important to send a thank-you letter or note to the reporter, with copies to his or her boss, especially if it was well done and accurate.

Obtain clippings or tapes for your files and keep a record of all interviews as a part of your evaluation efforts. You can get circulation figures from magazines and newspapers, and the producers of public affairs and news shows can give you ballpark figures of number of viewers. (Don't call the sales departments in radio and TV or you will get "shares" and "households" and you probably won't know how to translate those figures.) Keep good records on where your organization receives publicity and note any reaction or response you get from that coverage.

Because public relations is usually an intangible revenue generator, it is important to show the number of impressions you make in your community through your media interviews in order to judge the impact of your PR efforts (see Chapter 10, Why Should I Evaluate My PR Efforts?). Keep this important tracking information on the record and let me repeat: nothing you say to a reporter should ever be considered off the record.

Why Is the "Look" Important?

· 6 ·

The look of your agency's materials is important!

Did you know that a single piece of paper can "speak" for an organization? You should consider anything you or your colleagues put on paper that will be distributed to the public as speaking for the organization. Understand that those pieces of paper do, in fact, speak volumes. They can shout: "Small nonprofit with a copy machine and a little old lady in tennis shoes printing flyers on colored paper." Or, they can proclaim: "Serious, not-for-profit organization that is professional and effective." Obviously, you would prefer the latter.

Evaluating Your Agency's Printed Materials

If you represent an organization that is concerned with preserving a nature garden, you want to produce a brochure to explain the project and encourage donations. An ad agency agrees to design materials *pro bono*. The brochure they produce is gorgeous. With professional color photographs of the nature garden, the brochure unfolds into the shape of a tree! Very effective. Is it? Or does this piece scream "expensive!" Will donors fear their money may be paying more for the brochure than for programs to preserve the nature garden?

Let's examine ways the look of your agency's material can be of great benefit without costing a fortune. Write down everything you print. Here's a list to jog your memory:

Newsletter	Agency logo
Fact sheet	Press release paper
Brochure(s)	Fax forms
Annual report	Business cards
Annual conference materials	Letterhead

Envelopes   Program flyers
Certificates   Position papers awards
Posters   Invitations
Job applications   Signs
Training materials

Developing an Agency Logo

A good place to start is with the most visible symbol of any agency: the logo. If your organization doesn't have a logo, it should. The logo should be a registered trademark (which your agency's legal counsel can help you accomplish).

Have you ever seen the symbol that is on the POW/MIA flag? It is a bowed head in front of a guard tower, surrounded by barbed wire. That symbol is the logo of the National League of Families of American POWs and MIAs in Southeast Asia. The same symbol, however, is routinely used by many other organizations. Because the National League of Families never registered it as their trademark, the symbol is considered to be a part of the public domain and can be used by anyone. In this case, it isn't necessarily a bad thing since use of the symbol brings awareness to the overall issue of Americans who are still prisoners of war and missing in action in foreign countries. It would be quite different if any soda company could use the Coca Cola logo. It is in your agency's best interest to have its logo registered as a trademark.

A logo needs to be well thought out and graphically appealing. What will the symbol portray? Will the general public understand the meaning of your logo? Will it represent your agency well? This may be one of those times when you should consider hiring a graphic designer (see Chapter 8, When Should I Consider Outside Help?).

Once you have agreed upon a concept for an agency logo, you must decide if it will be printed in specific colors and if the typeface will always be the same. I personally believe it is important that your logo always be shown in the same font and color. Think about the blue IBM logo or the K-mart symbol. They are always the same and easily recognized. And who doesn't know what lies beneath the "golden arches"? The Alliance Theatre in Atlanta has a large stylized "A" as its logo. It is structured so you can also see a "T" in the logo. It is simple yet creative and instantly recognized.

Be aware of what your design looks like when printed in black and white. Some print media only use black and white. You must also be careful with your design. I saw a logo once for a botanical garden. It was a beautiful, stylized drawing of a lily-type flower in blue and purple. The

> It is in your agency's best interest to have its logo registered as a trademark. ■

first moment I looked at that logo I saw a medical drawing of a woman's reproductive organs. When I showed it to other people, some saw the same thing and some didn't. If that had been my organization and even one other person had seen the logo in that way, I would have changed it immediately.

When the design decision is made, have the logo represented in several different sizes and place them on one 8 1/2 x 11 sheet of paper to be printed on coated stock. This is now relatively easy to do on your computer, or a printer or quick copy shop can produce a ream (five hundred pages—the amount in a standard packet of paper) of these logo sheets for a relatively small charge. The logo sheets can then be used as camera-ready artwork for printed pieces (brochures, flyers) and for third parties who request a logo (like the sponsors of a 5K race benefiting your agency who want to put your logo on the race T-shirts). Logo sheets can also be placed in general agency press kits for media use.

You should also have the logo available on the computer so it can be transmitted electronically or on disk. This will make it easier for the many printers and publications that work directly from a disk or prefer to receive a copy of your logo by e-mail.

Now, look at all your agency's printed material and be sure the logo is on everything. You can have the most effective logo in the world, but if you forget to put it on your agency brochure or business cards or website, it won't do the organization much good.

To get an idea of how your agency materials look to the public, take all your printed material (from newsletters to business cards, brochures and training materials) and arrange them on a table or put everything on a bulletin board. Look carefully at this display. What do you see? Does the material look like a bunch of unrelated "stuff"? Or does it have a consistent look that makes it obvious that it is all part of one organization? If you just have "stuff," you need to make some changes. Having all your materials easily identifiable as belonging to the XYZ agency can be achieved through simple design techniques, color, and type style.

Coordinating Your "Look"

If you decide you do need to move toward a more coordinated look, it really isn't necessary to just toss all the old material into the recycle bin. Plan to replace each piece with the new design as supplies run out. Most nonprofits simply can't afford to get rid of large quantities of printed materials because they want to make a design change. Plan ahead for your new look. It may take you a year to fully complete the new look, but it will be worth the wait.

> ■ Have the logo available on the computer so it can be transmitted electronically or on disk.

> ■ Having all your materials easily identifiable as belonging to the XYZ agency can be achieved through simple design techniques, color, and type style.

As you work toward your consistent, coordinated "look," think about different typestyles and colors. As mentioned, I think it is a good idea to adopt a "corporate color" and have a designated typeface for your logo. Choose a color that will reproduce well and pick a typeface that is easy to read and common enough so that most computer programs and printers will have ready access to it. That concept can be carried into other materials. Just remember that whatever design you use, you may have to live with it for a long time.

Good design techniques tie your materials together. Use the same design with different colors for each piece, use the same color but with a different photograph or drawing, or use a template technique for each program or service offered by your agency and just pop copy and graphics into each printed piece.

If there is no one on the staff of your agency with graphic design experience, consider spending the money to hire freelance help. A good design concept is essential because these publications will represent your agency to the public. If there is absolutely no budget for freelance help, see if someone on the board of directors will underwrite the cost through his or her company as a donation. Investigate a trade-out for services, memberships, or tickets and offer a credit line for the designer ("This brochure designed *pro bono* by Neal & Associates"). There are some graphic designers who are new in their freelance business—trying to build a portfolio—who will donate their services for a credit line and your referrals for future business.

If push totally comes to shove, do the designing on your computer's desktop publishing program. Be careful. Desktop publishing is a wonderful invention that has saved nonprofits a lot of money. In the wrong hands, however, this modern technology can work against you if you do not use good design techniques. You don't want to hear comments like, "Oh, look, Save the Snails got a new computer program!" or "We used that same computer template for our brochure."

One good technique for producing readable, clean printed pieces is the effective use of white space. Repeat three times: "White space is my friend." Here's why:

Repeat three times: "White space is my friend." ■

> The Similar Syndromes Foundation (S.S.F.) provides counseling services for newly diagnosed patients, referrals to physicians specializing in the Similar Syndrome disorder, and a monthly newsletter containing current research and treatment options. For more information call 555-1234. There are no charges for services. Calls are confidential. S.S.F. is a nonprofit organization dedicated to helping people.

Human beings are funny creatures—they see all that writing and think it is too much to read and digest. So, we have to trick them into reading our message by putting it into smaller, more manageable bites. Use larger margins, put information into bullet form, and bump up the point size of the type to make the information easier to read.

> The Similar Syndromes Foundation (S.S.F.) provides services for newly diagnosed patients, including
> • Counseling
> • Referrals to physicians specializing in Similar Syndrome disorder
> • A monthly newsletter
>
> The mission of S.S.F. is to provide concerned people with information containing current research advances and treatment options.
>
> For more information call 555-1234. There are no charges for services.
>
> All calls are confidential. S.S.F. is a nonprofit organization dedicated to helping people.

Another basic element to consider in design concept is the color of the ink. Black ink is easy to read. Printing a brochure on sea foam green paper with pale blue ink may convey the "cool" feeling you want to communicate, but it will be very difficult to read. While the public may think your agency is cool, they won't have a clue what you do!

Which brings me back to my colored paper pet peeve. Using colored paper can be an effective technique for many materials like flyers, conference worksheets, and office memos, but get a grip, folks. Copying everything on goldenrod or red paper really does scream "This isn't serious" at your public.

Study the materials used by for-profit businesses and really notice the design. Obviously, large corporations have more money to spend on publications, but some of the design techniques can be adapted. To make materials stand out:
• Use design techniques like spot color, definition lines, and clip art.
• Pay attention to type styles, word and line spacing, placement on the page, use of colors and screens, and how photographs or drawings are used.

If you or someone on your staff will be responsible for designing publications, invest in a course on desktop publishing. Watch for inexpensive classes offered by college evening adult programs or local computer schools. If you absolutely have to do it yourself, ask for tips from someone who is more experienced with desktop publishing.

Another investment of time that will pay tremendous dividends is developing a good relationship with a printer. Printing terms can be intimidating—bleeds and die cuts, half tones, electronic production, and scans. I worked with one printer who provided a handy list of terms and definitions for his customers. A good printing sales representative can guide you through this confusion, help you find inexpensive paper, and explain how printing ten thousand brochures now is more cost effective than printing five thousand now and five thousand later.

A good way to keep your organization's look consistent and professional is to establish a method for quality control. Insist that everything, from flyers to brochures to grant proposals, be approved by you or someone on your staff. Proofread and check each piece for readability. Even if it is a grant proposal, the way it looks on the page will make it more professional, easier to read, and more compelling.

The look you send out to the public is an important aspect of a good public relations program. It can make the difference in perception of your agency's professionalism, whether or not a grant is approved, or how many members or volunteers you are able to recruit. In this area, a public relations generalist needs to be smart enough to know when outside help is needed, but creative enough to figure out how to get that help even if there is no money budgeted for it.

> Another investment of time that will pay tremendous dividends is developing a good relationship with a printer.

What Publications Do I Need?

· 7 ·

There are many different kinds of publications that benefit nonprofit organizations in public awareness efforts, fundraising, direct services, and volunteer recruitment. It would be difficult to pick "the" most important one. There are, however, some documents that should be at the top of the list. These include the annual report, agency newsletter, general brochure, and letterhead and business cards.

Annual Report

The annual report is an essential document for your agency because it serves so many purposes, such as:
- Soliciting corporate donations
- Providing easy reference for the media
- Filling requests for general information from state legislators
- Giving the board of directors a concise, fiscal year-end report

The annual report contains the most complete information about a nonprofit organization in one publication. It is the one piece that can communicate to all of your audiences.

Although it may seem intimidating, publishing an annual report is really not difficult. The hardest part will probably be getting the information from others in your agency to include in the report. You may also find that it is difficult to make staff understand that you are putting together a document about one specific fiscal year. If that year ended last June 30, they can't be giving you information about an event that occurred the following September. Another challenge for you will be to get the financial information from your agency's auditors in a timely manner. But you know best how to nag, beg, or threaten staff to get the information needed to write an annual report.

The bigger concern is to make sure people will want to read it. To get an idea of what kind of report might spark the imagination of your audiences, I suggest you start a file of copies of annual reports from other organizations—both for-profit and nonprofit. Your executive director probably receives copies of other organizations' reports—ask that these be routed on to you. Study these publications to get ideas on layout, design, use of colors, photographs, and writing styles. Notice what you like and what captures your imagination. Pay attention to what you think would and wouldn't work for your agency. Feel free to morph ideas that might work into your report.

I once came across an annual report from a major corporation that I assumed would be dull and boring. But some clever soul took photos of the top executives presenting reports in the book dressed for their favorite hobby or sport—gardening, tennis, rafting. It was just the right amount of levity I needed to actually compel me to read what these business executives had to say! Always keep in mind the nature of your organization, however. This kind of idea wouldn't work for an agency dealing with a deadly disease, for example.

Try to imagine how your annual report, as a standalone document, helps explain what your agency does. Let your mind go and think about something really different and creative.

- The Center for Puppetry Arts needed to produce an annual report on a limited budget. To save money and get people's attention, the publication was not bound like traditional annual reports but tied with marionette string.
- An environmental organization can print an annual report on paper made from recycled blue jeans or even flowers.
- A child-serving agency uses actual drawings by children for the graphics in its report.
- A school designs its report in the style of the old "Dick and Jane" readers.

As you look at a number of different annual reports, you should notice that the basic components of most of them are similar. Most will contain the following:

- Focused message from the board of directors' chair and/or executive director
- Brief history of the organization and the mission statement
- General description of each service the agency provides
- Accomplishments made during the previous fiscal year
- Lists of board members, major donors, volunteers, and staff
- Audited financial statement

You must have a budget for your annual report. Even if creative services are donated by a freelance graphic designer or public relations agency, there are still costs involved in producing the book, such as paper, printing, halftones, and binding. Most of these costs will be impacted by how many copies you print, namely the larger the print run (and thus final cost), the less cost per copy. Check carefully; you may find you can print extras for very little cost.

How many copies?

- Determine the number of reports you will need by deciding who will receive a copy—media, board members, association members, supporters, potential donors, and volunteers.
- Think about how many extra copies will be needed to last during the year for press kits, grant proposals, fundraising efforts, new board members, or volunteer orientations.

Talk to a printer

- Will the printer agree to print the piece at his cost if you guarantee him the contract to print your newsletter for a year?
- Can you afford color? What about the size of the piece and the weight of the paper? All of these are design components that will affect the cost.

Cost of mailing and storage

- The design can also impact the cost of mailing the report. If the report is designed to be oversized and will require special envelopes and additional postage, this must be calculated into your budget.
- And what about storing extra copies of the book? Ask your printer if copies can be stored in his warehouse free of charge. This is particularly important if your facility has limited storage space in the office.
- Know how the piece will be mailed and by whom (a mailing house or your own volunteers) before printing so you can print the correct bulk mail indicia on the outside if it is mailed without an envelope.

Whew—that's a lot to think about! Even when you have straightened out all of the above, designed a wonderful annual report, and written brilliant copy, you must remember to insist upon a press check. You need to be at the printer's facility when the first few copies of your annual report come off the press to make sure the pages are printed in the proper order and that the color is right. If a professional designer or writer is helping with this project, that person can also assist with the press check. If you are on your own, the printer is usually very helpful.

I learned to do press checks the hard way. I designed what I consid-

■ Insist upon a press check.

ered a gorgeous annual report for an agency. An ad agency shot powerful black-and-white photos *pro bono* for the book. The photos were placed full page on the left side of an 8 1/2 x 11 booklet-size piece. Copy was carefully laid out on the right-hand pages—with plenty of white space. I was so proud of my work, and the staff agreed it was a great design that worked well within our black-and-white budget. When the boxes of books arrived in the office, I excitedly retrieved the first copy and opened it to find that the printer had reversed the photos—they were placed on the *right side*! It ruined the entire design effect. Had I taken the time to do a press check, I would have caught this mistake.

Always do a press check!

Newsletter

A well-written, easy-to-read, attractive newsletter is a good way to keep communication flowing to your organization's constituents—board members, volunteers, members, media, donors, and sponsors. Whether this publication is quarterly or monthly, it provides a forum that can:

- Let readers know about current programs
- Promote upcoming events
- Spotlight volunteers
- List major donors
- Feature an educational area

After you and your executive director decide what should be in the agency newsletter, producing it becomes your task. Design is important. But the good thing about a newsletter is that once you have a design template, you can use it for each issue. Once the design is decided upon, it is useful to develop a timeline for producing the newsletter. If it is quarterly (which is the format most nonprofits use), your timeline might look like this:

January 15	Memo to staff for information to include in newsletter
January 30	All material due in PR office
February 7	First draft completed and sent to staff for proofreading
February 10	Changes due back in PR office
February 15	Deliver to printer for typesetting or start desktop publishing
February 17	Camera-ready newsletter ready for printing
February 18	Labels and postage delivered to mail house

> A well-written, easy-to-read, attractive newsletter is a good way to keep communication flowing to your organization's constituents.

February 24   Newsletters printed, folded
February 25   Newsletters delivered to mail house
March 1   Newsletters mailed bulk mail

I always found that a timeline helped keep me on schedule so that my quarterly newsletters were actually published in March, June, September, and December, the dates we had promised members they could expect to receive their copies.

When you are writing the newsletter, try to think about what you would want to read. As I've stated before, stay away from agency jargon. Try to make your copy sparkle by finding different ways to say things.

> Susan Jones attended the Similar Syndromes Foundation's first annual meeting in New Orleans to speak about being the first S.S. patient to receive a new therapy. Her speech was well received.

Boring! How about:

> Susan Jones, a vivacious 24-year-old Similar Syndrome patient, captured the attention of the audience at the opening session of the first S.S.F. annual meeting with a riveting speech. Susan, the first S.S. patient to receive the new biofeedback therapy, spoke passionately about the difference the therapy made in her life, including, she believes, making it possible for her to finish college. Susan's firsthand testimony resulted in an overflow crowd at the subsequent session that presented a panel to discuss the details of biofeedback therapy.

Another tip for a successful newsletter is to use good graphics and plenty of them. Have a photo of Susan at the annual meeting. If you attend the meeting, take a camera and get a good shot of this young woman gesturing during her speech. Use close-up shots and watch the background: you don't want a palm tree in the background to appear to be growing out of Susan's head!

If your newsletter goes to members, donors, or potential donors, you might want to use an inserted donor envelope in each issue. A simple envelope can be preprinted with something like, "Yes, I want to continue my support of the Similar Syndromes Foundation. Here is my donation to be used for research into the new biofeedback therapy." In the next issue, you might want to target the donations to a fund for a once-a-year retreat for S.S. patients and their families.

Besides the writing and printing of your newsletter, be prepared ahead of time for the most cost-efficient method for mailing. Here are some things to double-check:

- If the publication is designed as a self-mailer and sent bulk mail, check with the post office prior to printing for the most current regulations about what size it can be, where the return address should be placed, and if using bar codes will lower your costs.
- Always request that bad addresses be returned to you. Just as media lists have to be constantly updated, so do your newsletter mailing lists. In the three months between newsletters, one fourth of your recipients could have moved! You will have to pay postage on returned items, but it is worth it to keep your mailing list up-to-date.
- If the newsletter will be sent bulk mail, I believe it is well worth the money to have a mail house do your mailing. A good mail house can earn their fee from the money they save your organization in postage. Because this is their profession, they stay up-to-date on current regulations and can suggest ways to bundle newsletters to take advantage of the lowest postal rates.

Aren't you glad you only have to do this four times a year?

Brochure

A general agency brochure is also a vital document. This publication is different from an annual report in several ways. It isn't as extensive or detailed, it doesn't carry a financial statement, and it is generally distributed to a more widespread audience, many of whom aren't aware of your organization.

The kind of brochure you produce will depend on what kind of nonprofit agency you represent. You should consider carefully the audience your brochure will reach and then tailor the content—both words and graphics—to that audience. A zoo or museum needs a brochure that uses colorful, dynamic graphics and copy to compel people to visit. A disease-related agency may need a brochure that notes the symptoms of the condition, available treatments, and services provided by the organization to help patients. The look of this piece will be more serious. It needs to be designed as a quick reference about the disease with easy-to-find telephone numbers and addresses. A humane society brochure should list local facts about abandoned animals with magnificent photos of dogs and cats wanting homes. Testimonials from happy new pet owners might help as well, along with the obvious listing of specific

Just as media lists have to be constantly updated, so do your newsletter mailing lists.

information about adoption sites and requirements for taking an animal home.

Remember our friend "white space" when designing a brochure and try not to be tempted to write more than people want to know. You live and breathe your organization every day, and you know much more information than the average person wants or needs to know. Step back and think about the few important points you need to include in the brochure to get people to visit your facility, to contact the agency for more detailed information, to adopt an animal, to join your church choir, or to get tested for AIDS.

Letterhead and Business Cards

Letterhead and business cards sometimes get lost in the shuffle when thinking about "publications." Remember that the business card you give to someone and the letterhead you use for correspondence represent your organization as much as the annual report or brochure.

Design a letterhead that uses your logo well and contains pertinent information but isn't busy. Don't try to include the mailing address, street address, website address, e-mail address, telephone number, fax number, and cell phone number all on the letterhead. Keep it simple.

Some organizations have different styles of letterhead for different purposes:

- A letterhead printed on high-quality paper with the logo in color for special correspondence
- A general black-and-white letterhead for routine correspondence
- A letterhead with the board of directors or trustees printed down the side for donor solicitation letters or grant requests

With the exception of the last example, try to avoid designing a letterhead that forces people to reset the margins on their word processing programs. Be sure to have appropriate-size envelopes and second sheets for the letterhead, and print stick-on address labels to use for large envelopes and boxes.

Business cards should also be kept simple. Resist the temptation to be cute. I personally don't like business cards that are folded or printed vertically. A simple, professional look on standard-size business cards works well. Include the agency logo, address, phone, fax, and website. Here you may want to use your e-mail address and cell phone number if that is appropriate for your job. Don't forget the name and correct title of the person for whom the business card is being printed. A little internal PR tip: when a new employee joins the staff, it's a nice touch to have business cards printed and waiting on his or her first day.

I believe that printed material is an area where nonprofits should not be penny-wise and pound-foolish. Make sure there is quality control for all printed material. Maintain a consistent, coordinated "look" for all material. Educate yourself about printing. Learn to know when you need the help of a professional!

Put as much time, energy, and thought into the creation of your printed material as you put into the creation of your services and programs.

When Should I Consider Outside Help?

· 8 ·

Several times in this book you will see references to freelance writers, graphic designers, trainers, or consultants. Perhaps their role in your nonprofit organization needs to be better defined. Who are these people, what do they do, and why would your organization need them?

A consultant is someone who, for whatever reason, is considered an "expert" in a particular field. A consultant with vast knowledge and experience helps you accomplish a task that is outside your area of expertise by guiding you through that task.

For example, you are stuck trying to create a year-long public relations plan. Because this was not your course of study in school (or because you have never practiced PR before) you simply don't have the background and experience to know how to craft the best plan. So, you contact a public relations, marketing, or communications consultant who can help you get started or look at what you have done so far and make suggestions on how to improve the plan.

Consultants are usually advisors, not doers. Having said that, fourteen consultants will now pop up and tell me I'm wrong. But if a consultant is also the doer, isn't he or she actually a freelance practitioner? It's all too confusing, so let's go with my premise that consultants merely consult and leave the "doing" to you.

Your consultant will probably meet with you and ask questions about what your agency's goals are, how much budget you have in specific areas (like printing and promotion), and what staff and volunteer resources you have. Then, ideas and suggestions will be offered so you can write a more effective plan. Consultants usually charge an hourly fee, although some may charge on a project basis.

A freelance public relations or communications practitioner, on the other hand, will actually do the work for you—for a fee. After learning about your organization and its goals for its public relations plan, this individual will actually create the plan for you. These services are not inexpensive but may well be worth the expenditure to have an effective PR plan for your organization. Freelancers also charge by the hour or by the project. In some rare cases, you may be able to find someone who will work *pro bono* or will trade out his services for tickets, merchandise, or services offered by your agency.

If you don't have a person on staff who can create graphic images or manage desktop publishing effectively, you may need to find a freelance graphic designer. For the layout of a quarterly newsletter, most freelance graphics designers use a computer to "typeset" a newsletter and create camera-ready artwork that can be placed on a disk for the printer to use. If you are changing your brochures to have a more modern and coordinated look, a designer can be of tremendous help with concept, design, and layout. A good graphics person can help design a logo, if for some reason your organization doesn't have one or if there is a need to change the existing logo. A freelancer can also design signage, special event T-shirts, bumper stickers, and agency stationery. Graphic designers work on an hourly or per-project fee basis.

Freelance writers can also be very useful for special projects. If you are changing or updating brochures and can find the money in your budget, outsourcing the writing of the brochure may be a good idea. You will be surprised how much help a "fresh eye" can be. If you have been working for your organization for five years and honestly can't think of a new way to say "The Similar Syndromes Foundation helps people who are sick," a freelance writer might come up with "The Similar Syndromes Foundation (S.S.F.) is unique in the nonprofit world because it assists people who face daily life battling a spectrum of illnesses not always recognized or diagnosed by the medical profession. S.S.F. enhances the quality of life for these people by providing valuable information and tips about these illnesses, how to cope, and how to find a doctor qualified to treat this unusual group of ailments."

If you have never prepared an annual report and get hives just thinking about it, a freelance writer can do that job for you. However, the hardest part of an annual report is usually gathering the information from all the various departments in your agency. If you plan to do that part of the job anyway, you might as well take a stab at writing the report. Maybe the freelancer's role is to edit what you write and give it some sparkle. Most writers charge by the hour and aren't inexpensive. In some cases, however, it is money very well spent, especially if writing is not your strong suit.

Just as the look of your materials is important (see Chapter 6, Why Is the 'Look' Important?), so are the words contained in your publications. You want those words to motivate, captivate, compel, touch hearts, and speak to the people reading them. In some cases, it is just smart to hire someone whose expertise is writing. Try to evaluate how much time it would take you to write something and calculate what your salary would be for that effort. If it is an eight-hour effort, figure those hours at your hourly salary rate. Then, look at what else you could be doing in that time that would be more productive. It may be that the eight hours you spend gathering information for case histories to use for media requests is much more valuable. When you look at it from that perspective, the freelancer's fee doesn't seem so steep.

A trainer is someone who teaches you and/or staff and volunteers how to do something better. (We discussed media training in Chapter 4, Why Must I Have Media Relations?) Media training is a good example of spending a little money to reap large rewards. Responding well to the media and giving better media interviews can only benefit your organization.

An organization that deals with the public on a routine basis, such as a museum, theatre, or nonprofit educational institution, might consider training in CPR and first aid to be very beneficial.

If you represent an organization that routinely deals with the public, you might also consider customer service training for both staff and volunteers. First impressions are so important. If your donors or clients are treated poorly on the telephone or in person, they will always remember that and will tell others about their negative experience. Since word of mouth is one of the most valuable publicity tools for some organizations, you certainly don't want people out there bad-mouthing you. Investing in annual or semiannual customer service training may be well worth the bucks!

We will discuss websites later in this book (Chapter 15, Where Is My Website?). For most organizations, this is an area that requires outside help. It is important that your agency's website be carefully planned and executed. Fees vary for this service. As a nonprofit, it is possible to find a technology company or web service that will donate a site to your organization.

Think about the kinds of things you might use outside help to accomplish. The most obvious outsourcing for almost all nonprofits is printing. Unless you are a huge national charity and have your own print shop, you send pieces to a printer. (We discussed printers a bit in Chapter 6, Why Is the 'Look' Important?) Printers charge by the job.

Estimates for the same job by different printers can vary widely. If you are looking for a printer for your quarterly newsletter, get at least three estimates and ask for references. You can also negotiate. I have been successful at asking a printer to produce the first newsletter for free if I guarantee the other three newsletters will go to that printer for the rest of the year. That saves one fourth of the budget for printing the newsletter and gives the printer known income for the coming year. Ask your printer if there is a less expensive paper similar to the one you would like to use for the newsletter. A good printer will be happy to work with you to try to keep costs low.

There are many ways that freelancers, trainers, and consultants can help your organization communicate better and present professional printed pieces to your audience. Finding the right person for the job is important.

- Contact the nearest chapter of the Public Relations Society of America to see if they have listings of freelancers and consultants.
- Check out the Internet using the keywords "freelance writers."
- You can put an ad in the newspaper, but this can be a double-edged sword, creating more work just combing through resumés.
- Sometimes it is best to contact a few colleagues at other organizations. Talk to Jane Smith at Save the Snails and see if she has worked with someone who did a great job at a fair price.

When you have identified someone who meets your needs, ask for references and check them. Take a close look at the person's portfolio. If a graphic designer's work seems to have odd typefaces or quirky design techniques, maybe he or she isn't appropriate for your agency. You also need to make the time frames and deadlines clear for any given project. Get fee structures in writing and determine when payment is due. If the freelancer asks for full pay up front, find someone else. You might, however, agree to pay a deposit (stipulating that it is refundable if the work isn't completed accurately or on time), with full payment due immediately upon completion of the project or thirty days thereafter. Do remember that freelancers often spend a great deal of time trying to collect fees. Be conscientious and pay them when the payment is due.

Once you have found a freelancer or consultant who fits with your organization, the benefits can be tremendous. If you use the same writer a couple of times a year, that person already knows about your agency and doesn't have to be reoriented each time.

I once used a freelancer for a yearly brochure that was time consum-

> Finding the right free-
> lancer, trainer, or con-
> sultant for the job is
> important.

ing and just a horrible piece to put together. She had worked with my organization for several years and was knowledgeable about what we did, the purpose of this brochure, and when it had to be completed. She did such an outstanding job that even after she moved eight hundred miles away, we kept using her for that project. Telephones, fax machines, and computers are wonderful tools!

Sometimes spending money on outside assistance will reap incredible rewards for your organization. However, you do need to be able to convince your executive director and/or board chair of the benefit. Be prepared to defend your request with good research on staff time usage versus the dollars spent for outsourcing. While outside help can be a godsend, be careful. If you find that you are depending upon freelancers and consultants more and more, maybe it is time to do some number crunching and convince the powers that be that it's time to hire a part-time person to complete those projects as a staff member.

Sometimes spending money on outside assistance will reap incredible rewards for your organization.

What's So Special about Special Events?

· 9 ·

In the early 1980s, I struggled to help keep public awareness high for Americans still missing in action and prisoner of war in Southeast Asia. The Vietnam War was not popular. The country was relieved when "Operation Homecoming" returned nearly six hundred prisoners of war to the United States. The end of the war was in sight. The soldiers were home and the country tried to "get back to normal" after seeing body bags and casualty counts on the evening news for years. I was tasked with keeping awareness high about those soldiers who hadn't come home—not an easy task for a topic no one wanted to talk about! To try to quell many unanswered questions and the frustrations of the families of the twenty-five hundred Americans still missing in Southeast Asia, Congress decreed that National POW/MIA Recognition Day be held each year to honor and pay tribute to former POWs and to the families of the missing soldiers.

One year, I decided to coordinate the release of twenty-five hundred balloons across the country on POW/MIA Recognition Day. This task was not as difficult as you might think because my job was to work with groups throughout the United States dedicated to the issue of Americans still missing. Through my regular communication channels, I recommended the project, provided "how to" instructions, kept a list of where ceremonies were planned, and coordinated publicity.

Over three hundred locations from Florida to Alaska participated in this very special event. Because of the impressive number of releases scheduled, the national headquarters of my organization was able to convince the White House press office to include this activity in the speech the president made at the national ceremony in Washington, D.C., on POW/MIA Recognition Day. That added special significance to this event and helped make discussion of the POW/MIA issue a little easier for me and for the groups across the country working for a full accounting of American personnel. (Note: Today, balloon releases are not acceptable because we know that all those balloons come down somewhere and damage the environment in some way—from clogging streams to being eaten by animals, whose digestive systems can't tolerate latex balloons. Large balloon releases are not appropriate for special events today!)

Your special event will probably be more focused in the local, maybe regional, area. However, the challenges and opportunities of a special event for your organization will be similar.

A good starting point for discussing special events is to identify the purpose of that event. What would possibly motivate you and your organization to go to all that trouble to hold a fun run or a quilting contest or a middle school art contest or an apple pie bake-off? It is probably because you want to bring attention to an important aspect of the work your agency does on a day-to-day basis. You may need to bring awareness to an urgent social issue or lay the groundwork for an upcoming fundraising effort or countywide immunization drive. Like anything you do in the name of the organization you represent, special events should be considered a way to impact your public and each event must be planned with the utmost attention to detail.

Planning is essential for a successful special event. Allowing enough time for the planning and implementation process is equally important. I find it interesting that people will plan their weddings six months to a year in advance but may decide that in a month they will hold a carnival and silent auction for their church. Most larger nonprofits that hold an annual gala fundraising event, like a black-tie ball, start planning next year's event the day after this year's event takes place.

The best way to illustrate how to plan for a special event is to actually go through the process. So let's plan an event! The Similar Syndromes Foundation is going to host a barbecue picnic and silent auction as both an awareness event and a fundraiser. Take a deep breath and let's go.

People organize in different ways. Some prefer a large wall chart to visually present all aspects of an event. Others like a three-ring notebook divided into committee sections. I prefer to simply start a file and work from a series of checklists. As the file grows, I divide it out into several files (e.g., volunteers, publicity, food). I often keep the files spread out on a separate table or in a standing file holder on my desk. You might prefer using an electronic calendar on your computer or one of the handheld electronic organizers. It doesn't matter how you do it as long as you start off organized and stay that way throughout the entire process.

> Planning is essential for a successful special event. Allowing enough time for the planning and implementation process is equally important.

> The first step in planning any event is to choose an active, involved committee to help put the event together with staff. The committee's first task is to decide on a date, time, and location.

The first step in planning any event is to choose an active, involved committee to help put the event together with staff. The committee's first task is to decide on a date, time, and location. If you are in an area where there are many charitable events, try to determine a date that will not conflict with the humane society's bark-off or the symphony's annual ball. In larger areas, the city magazine or lifestyle section of the newspaper may list events planned for the next four to six months. I worked on one event that was planned each year so it would not coincide with a particular university's football games because so many board members were alumni and attended all of the games. That seems like a small, silly detail, but it was very serious to those board members who cared—and who were very important to the effort of selling tables at this event.

In most areas, special events tend to cluster in the fall, around the holidays, and in the spring. S.S.F. decided to do something different with its barbecue. Why not hold it in late January when the holidays are over and (in most areas of the country) everyone is in the winter doldrums? That gives the planning committee eight months, which should be enough time to create a great event. Let's recommend that S.S.F. schedule the time for the event from noon to 5:00 P.M. What about a name for the event? Sometimes a clever name will help promote the event. After some brainstorming, the S.S.F. staff and event chairperson decide to call it the first annual Winter Barbecue Festival.

Now the push is on to find a location for the festival. In January, it should be an indoor venue. That could be fun—a barbecue indoors in January! Special consideration will have to be made for using grills indoors. That could be tricky, but I know where the event can be held. The high school has a cafetorium adjacent to a sheltered, porchlike area where students are allowed to have their lunch in good weather. S.S.F. can let the hardy souls who volunteer to cook use the outside area (the grills will generate good heat) and they can set up to serve inside. The silent auction can be set up on the stage area at the end of the cafetorium. This could work!

The planning committee now needs to contact the school and meet with the principal to discuss the project. They will stress that volunteers will not impact regular school functions. If permitted, setup will begin Friday evening and cleanup will be completed by Sunday evening. As compensation for using the school's facility, S.S.F. will offer to pay a flat rental fee or suggest that a donation of a percentage of the profits from the event go to the school to help cover the overhead costs—such as electricity and gas for cooking on their stoves.

So far, my file looks like this:

S.S.F. Fundraiser:
Date: Saturday, January 25th
Time: Noon–5:00 P.M.
Place: Anywhere, USA High School
Ample free parking
P. A. system in place
Tables and chairs available for eating and for the silent auction
Kitchen area for food preparation and cleanup
Outdoor space for grills

Next, S.S.F. and the planning committee must set up the subcommittees that will be necessary to plan and implement the event. Staff must call on already-established volunteers or recruit new or additional volunteers. Perhaps the high school where the event is scheduled to take place has a youth service organization that would like to use the event to fulfill community service requirements. For this kind of event, the staff and the event chairperson might set up the following committees: publicity, silent auction, finance, site coordination, food, entertainment, cleanup, and thank-you. It is helpful to outline some responsibilities and timelines ahead of time and hand this information to the person who agrees to be the volunteer in charge of each area.

Sample Responsibilities and Timeline

Chairperson
   1. This volunteer will serve as the spokesperson for S.S.F. and this event in media interviews.

   2. The chairperson will hold regular meetings to discuss the status of plans and to ensure that all committees are functioning well. The first meeting will be scheduled for July 15 and after that at the chair's pleasure.

   3. The chairperson and PR staff will maintain a master checklist for the event to monitor progress and make sure no detail is overlooked.

Publicity *(This may need to be a staff function)*
   1. This group is responsible for generating publicity about the event ahead of time, for stimulating ticket sales, and for promoting awareness about S.S.F.

2. The publicity chair is responsible for securing media coverage during the event and reporting on the success of the event. This volunteer will set up a timetable for press releases and for information for periodicals:
   • Periodical information mailed no later than October 30
   • Calendar notices disseminated January 2 to weekly and daily newspapers and radio
   • Media pitches sent to TV public affairs programs in early December
   • Media advisory for coverage of the event sent out a week prior
   • A public relations plan should be prepared with these and all other timelines by September 1st.

Silent Auction

Note: For those unfamiliar with silent auctions, the idea is to get items donated that will then be auctioned to the highest bidder. Items are displayed on tables with bid sheets and pencils. Throughout the event, guests are encouraged to review the auction items and write a bid. Everyone can see the previous bids and make his or her bid just a little higher.

In some areas, web auction companies are offering to hold an Internet auction at no charge to the nonprofit, which gets to keep all proceeds from the auction. This is a good marketing tool for the auction's website because it will drive traffic to the site from supporters of the charity, who might also browse through the site's paying clients.

1. The Silent Auction Chairperson should immediately draft a plan that includes where this committee will seek donations for the auction. For example:
   • Cultural attractions will usually donate a family pass
   • Restaurants will provide a dinner for two
   • An appliance store may donate a toaster oven
   • A jewelry store could provide a necklace
2. Think beyond the obvious items and seek out unusual things that will spark a bidding war—like a morning in the studio with a popular radio personality. Call on everyone on the board of directors for contacts at airlines for tickets, travel agencies for vacation packages, etc.
3. This committee is also responsible for closing the bidding before the end of the event, deciding the winning bids, and collecting money for the items. It will also make sure people who don't pick up their items at the event are notified about where to pick them up at a later date.

Finance Committee
1. This committee is responsible for setting a goal for the event: how much money do the volunteers reasonably think can be raised?
2. The volunteer chair must create a budget for expenses based on the expected revenue. Costs for the barbecue and other food items, printing of tickets, silent auction programs, signs, etc., should be taken into account.
3. This committee will also be responsible for selling tickets to the event and can assist the silent auction committee in collecting bid money during the event.
4. Works closely with S.S.F. accounting staff.

Site Coordination
1. This committee will make sure that the high school cafetorium is set up properly before the event, borrowing or renting any equipment not available at the school.
2. The setup and cleanup will follow school guidelines (i.e., if there are rules about not taping signs to the wall, someone will be assigned to make sure that doesn't happen).
3. Coordination with the food committee and cleanup committee will ensure that the site is treated with responsible care.
4. Volunteers will set up the tables and chairs and be responsible for taking them down after the event and returning them to their proper place.
5. Any special insurance information or fire codes will also be handled by this committee.

Food Committee
1. This really isn't as obvious as it seems. This committee will be responsible for buying, preparing, and serving the food. However, it is also in charge of estimating how much food is needed, safely handling meat, and following health codes. They will work with the finance committee to determine a charge for the meal that people will purchase to make sure it covers expenses and still contributes to profit.
2. This committee may want to recruit school cafetorium employees as volunteers to help with food preparation (or pay them a minimum stipend).
3. The volunteers on this committee pray the cleanup committee is able to recruit many helpers!

Entertainment
1. This committee finds entertainment, if that is a part of the plan. For a barbecue, a bluegrass band or a children's clogging group would be great.
2. The committee members negotiate a fee, make sure audio equipment is in place, and decide how many "sets" the band or performers will do.

Cleanup
The cleanup committee is crucial to the success of your event. If you want to make the event an annual gathering, be sure that when you leave, the cafetorium is spotless and ready for school to be in session on Monday.

Thank-You
1. Also an important part of your event organization, this committee makes sure all the companies that donated items to the silent auction receive a thank-you letter, a copy of any publicity that listed donors, and a letter for the company's tax file.
2. The thank-you volunteers also make sure all other volunteers and supporters are thanked in an appropriate way. When people do something to help a nonprofit organization, it is vitally important to thank them profusely for their help.

In addition to giving the committees their assignments, it is important for the chair and staff person to maintain a checklist for events. Include anything unusual that may not be covered in the committees. In the case of the barbecue, that included:
• Researching safe food handling for the food committee
• Determining how many parking spots were available in the parking lot and where to park any overflow
• Deciding what to do with leftover food
• Having procedures in place for dealing with lost children
• Having copies of the recipe for the barbecue sauce available for sale if appropriate
• Ensuring extra toilet paper is stored for use in the restrooms so you don't deplete the school's supply
An event checklist is your guide to make sure no one forgets anything. When the Getty Museum was built in Los Angeles, the facility was gorgeous, the exhibitions were divine, and the volunteers were all in place. A checklist might have alerted the powers that be to the fact that

plans for the museum did not include enough bathrooms for the anticipated number of visitors!

This bathroom theme isn't meant to be amusing. When nature calls, people aren't happy to have to wait. Remember that at most events you need twice as many women's restrooms as men's. In many facilities, it is possible to reassign men's rooms to ladies' rooms.

Think of anything that could possibly go wrong with your event and have an alternative plan. I went to a convention once in a beautiful new meeting center. There was a break in the pipe supplying the sprinkler system and it "rained" in the exhibition hall for forty-five minutes—on computers, on the meeting registration area, and on the caterers preparing the opening reception! Fortunately, the meeting planners had a Plan B, which involved immediately moving the food into the spacious lobby, booting up backup computers stored in another area of the center, and hiring help to clean up and reset the hall. The conference continued with as little disruption as could be in the case of an unplanned, indoor rainstorm.

S.S.F. is holding its barbecue in January, so let's think about what might go wrong:

- What if the S.S.F. headquarters is in Alabama, where it rarely snows, but there is a freak snowstorm? Should there be an alternative date in case of bad weather?
- What if the football team at the high school where you plan to hold the event wins the state championship and the only night they can hold their awards banquet is the same night as the S.S.F. event?

You get the idea—let your mind go wild and try to anticipate any potential problem. Then, create a Plan B for each scenario.

In this ever-changing world there is now something called "event insurance." You can actually take out an insurance policy for bad weather, stains on your wedding dress, or photos that don't come out! I know Fireman's Fund offers this kind of insurance and others are sure to follow.

Another important thing to consider is attendance. Obviously, if the event is a fundraiser, you want to make money. However, you also want to be a success by having people attend even if you are just doing an awareness day. I like to ensure a good audience.

My organization sponsored a lecture and book signing by an author from California who had written a book about the ocean. This wasn't really a fundraiser but part of a public awareness day. My staff did their part to publicize the event, had the facility ready, and made sure the audio equipment was working properly. The bookstore partnering with my organization was busy that same weekend with a major celebrity author in town for a book signing. Our author fell by the wayside—literally. No one from the bookstore remembered to pick him up at the airport! A total of two people at the event went into the theater to hear his presentation. It was so embarrassing.

The next time we hosted an author, it was someone who had written a book about the Mars mission in 1997. To make sure that my organization and the bookstore were not embarrassed for the author, we invited our own audience. Students from two nearby colleges were invited to attend free of charge so we were sure there would be people to listen to this interesting author present her story.

For the Winter Barbecue Festival, consider having the local children's choir as part of the entertainment. Invite one parent to attend for free when accompanied by a child. Other relatives will want to purchase tickets and attend the event to hear their little darling perform. Or you could have a ticket sales contest with prizes. And speaking of prizes, advertise door prizes at the event.

All your planning has been carefully done, it is a week before the festival, and you call all of your volunteers together for a walk-through at the school. Make sure all committees know what is expected of them during the setup process, while the event is actually taking place, and following the event.

- Look at each area to be sure there is enough room for tables, adequate lighting, and electrical plugs if needed.
- Make sure someone has arranged to have the heat turned on.
- Decide where guests will hang coats.
- Determine traffic flow to where food is being served, to the tables, and to silent auction items.
- Make sure audio equipment will not obstruct anyone's view of the master of ceremonies or entertainment.
- Be sure there is adequate parking and consider having someone direct traffic in the parking lot so no cars get blocked in.

That's it. Now you are ready to have a glorious event, raise lots of money, and have the community marvel at how clever it was to hold a barbecue in January!

A special event can be intimidating. The secret is to break it into pieces that are easier to handle. If you are the staff person ultimately responsible for the event, make sure you recruit enough volunteers to make the task more manageable. You may want to break your committees down even further so that each volunteer has only one or two tasks. Pay attention to detail, don't make assumptions about anything, and double-check everything!

Pay attention to detail, don't make assumptions about anything, and double-check everything!

Think about a special event for your organization as if it were your wedding or the wedding of your daughter. You want it to be perfect and the most memorable day in history. That takes good planning, good timing, and good organization. Good luck!

Why Should I Evaluate My PR Efforts?

·10·

Large corporations spend considerable time and resources evaluating their audiences and assessing the effectiveness of their marketing and advertising efforts. Evaluating public relations activity is a little more difficult and something that most nonprofits do not do. It is important, however, to determine which activities are most effective in accomplishing your goals and objectives. When you have a limited budget, you don't want to continue with tactics that aren't working.

There are procedures you can put into place that will give your agency better guidelines on which efforts work and which ones are a waste of time and resources. Please understand that I am not making clear, distinct differentiation between PR and marketing. Because of limited resources in nonprofits, you may have to lump everything together under the PR umbrella. Just the process of thinking about what public relations and/or marketing activities the organization does and how you might evaluate the success of those efforts can be revealing and helpful to future planning.

Some kind of evaluation technique should be included in every PR plan and as a part of any awareness activities. For example, do you mail a separate press release for everything your agency does—one for volunteer recruitment, one for new class schedules, one for a special event? For years, I was on the mailing list for a water park in Florida, probably because I was an accredited member of the Florida Public Relations Association. Every few weeks, I received a large envelope with a press release about one specific event and a lovely eight-by-ten glossy photograph. I had moved several times, including one move out of the state, and did not remain a good candidate for their press list. I got to the point where I didn't even open the envelopes and tossed them into the circular file under my desk. This organization was very good at keeping the addresses on their press list current, but they weren't good at evaluating my effectiveness as a media contact for them.

Think about how the recipient is reacting to your mailings. Are you sending too much information to the same people too often? Consider a quarterly press release (discussed in Chapter 3, Who, What, When, Where, and Why?) that incorporates a short background statement on your agency and a brief description of events and activities for the coming three months. Try to target your mailing more specifically. A volunteer recruitment press release will go to different media than an advisory on new research.

In Chapter 4, Why Must I Have Media Relations?, we discussed establishing a media guide. It is imperative to keep this guide, from which you build your media mailing list, updated at least every three months. Especially for nonprofits that have no money to waste, consider how it looks when media organizations get duplicate mailings, too many mailings, or material sent to someone who left that organization a year ago. What message does that send? Not a very professional one, I can assure you.

Do you rely on radio PSAs to get the word out about services provided? When do those PSAs actually air and who is really listening? (The radio station should be able to give you a listing of when the spots ran.) Think about who is listening at 5:30 A.M. on a Sunday morning. Is that really your target audience? Is it worth the effort to prepare and mail material for those PSAs or would your limited staff resources be better spent in some other way?

After reviewing how you initiate and implement the agency's public relations program, there are some relatively simple things you can do to determine the impact your PR efforts have. An effective measurement can be to keep track of the "impressions" your agency makes in the community and to issue a quarterly report for staff and the board of directors. (Impressions are the sum of all exposures your message has through printed material, radio time, television spots, billboards, newspaper stories, distributed brochures, trade show booths, speeches to groups, etc.) Gathering information on the impact you are making in the community isn't as difficult as it sounds. Keep a running tab of all agency PR activities and lay out a report in three or four sections.

Section 1: Print Media
- If you live in a large area (and have the budget), employ a professional clipping service to scan all print publications in your city, region, or state for stories that mention your agency.

- If your city or town is small and/or there is no budget to pay for such a service, assign volunteers or staff to read the newspapers and any local magazines on a regular basis and clip stories.
- Make copies of the clippings and record the circulation of the publication. (Circulation figures can be obtained by calling newspaper or magazine subscription departments.)
- At the end of each year you may want to compile all of your clippings into a booklet that will serve as a record of your print media activity.

Section 2: Electronic Media
- Keep a running list of news stories on TV in which your organization was featured.
- Write down any public affairs radio or TV programs on which staff or volunteers were guests.
- In some larger cities there are also "clipping" services for television, but these are expensive. Instead, arrange for someone to tape the appearances on a VCR at home or in the office. Most radio stations are glad to make a cassette recording of interviews for you to keep.
- Call the promotion departments of the stations to get "ballpark" figures of viewers or listeners. (Don't contact the advertising departments because they will provide numbers for households and market share figures, and these will totally confuse most people. You simply want to know approximately how many human beings are tuned in.)

Section 3: Marketing or Community Outreach
- Keep track of all outreach efforts (including festivals, parades, or other community activities) at which your organization has a presence. These include making speeches to Kiwanis clubs, schools, and churches; having a booth at a trade show; or taking your agency mascot to a festival.
- Ask event organizers what the expected attendance is and use this figure for your report. For example, the local zoo takes several small animals from the petting zoo to the Baby and Kid Fair at the regional convention center as a way of reminding people to revisit the zoo. Organizers believe they will attract twenty thousand visitors in two days. Use that figure for your report— or reduce it proportionally if the agency can only staff a booth one day out of the two days of the expo. This isn't an exact sci-

ence, but it will give you a good indication of about how many people you are reaching.

Section 4: Advertising

- More and more nonprofits understand the value of advertising, whether it is paid for out of the agency's expense budget, is donated by a corporation, or is a trade-out with the media entity for products or services. If your organization is fortunate enough to be able to place ads in the local newspaper or on radio or television, use the same tracking techniques to determine how many people you reach. Find out the circulation figures or approximate number of viewers or listeners. Use those numbers in your report.

Prepare your report on a regular basis, perhaps quarterly, to evaluate how many people you are reaching through your communication efforts. It should be laid out so it looks good and is easy to read—just like all your other publications. There are many computer programs that lend themselves to this kind of report. A sample format is provided here.

Similar Syndromes Foundation Communication Report—First Quarter
(January, February, March)

Print Media	Circulation
January 3 Story on Holiday Cheer for Similar Syndrome patients *Anywhere, USA Daily Report*	25,000
January 19 Calendar announcement for volunteers *County Weekly Tabloid*	14,500
February 14 Feature story on Valentine social event Sunday edition of the *Daily Report*	57,000
March 4 Fundraising report in the city business weekly	8,200
Total Print Media for 1st Quarter	**104,700**

Electronic Media	Number of People
January 1 "New Year Brings Hope for S.S.F. Research" WXXI-TV, 6:00 News	15,600
February 14 Valentine's event covered by WBBB-TV 5:00, 11:00, and the next day at noon	41,000
February 24 Longtime S.S.F. volunteer interviewed on WAA FM Radio Public Affairs Program	12,000
March 2 Community "Headlights On Day" in support of March fundraising effort covered by WXXI-TV news in-depth on noon show	9,500
Total Electronic Media for 1st Quarter	**78,100**

Marketing/Community Outreach	Number of People
January 2 New Year Nonprofit Jamboree at the Convention Center	9,300
February 10 Speech to Kiwanis Club	120
February 19 Anywhere, USA Founder's Day Parade Float and S.S.F. ribbon distribution	7,600
March 5 S.S.F. awareness workshop at local hospital	210
Total Marketing Outreach for 1st Quarter	**17,230**

This gives you an idea of one way to evaluate your efforts. This can be an ongoing task for a loyal office volunteer, intern, or administrative support staff. Once you establish the report as routine, keep a running list of activities, and have the format on a computer; it is not very difficult or time-consuming. Once the report is compiled, provide copies to senior management and the board of directors to demonstrate the effectiveness of the agency's communication efforts.

There are, of course, other evaluation methods. Some are listed below to point you in the right direction:

Statistics

> Evaluate where members, volunteers, visitors, or program participants come from by zip code. Then look at what PR efforts were made in those areas.

Couponing

> If your agency is a performing arts center, museum, or other "attraction" that requires an admission fee (or runs a thrift shop or charges for workshops), the distribution of discount coupons works well. Coupons are collected by staff and then counted and tabulated once a month to determine which ones resulted in more traffic. If you distributed five hundred coupons through a local grocery store and fifty came back to you, that was pretty successful. If you put five hundred coupons at a local dry cleaner and two came back, you may want to reconsider that placement. Code your coupons so you will know where they were placed.

Surveys/Evaluation Forms

> Ask participants in classes, workshops, or special events to fill out a brief survey about their experience. This will provide you with valuable information and can be a way to build supporter mailing lists.

Focus Groups

> Bring small groups of your members, supporters, potential donors, or other targeted audiences to your facility for lunch and a discussion about programs and services. What are the perceptions of the agency? How do people find out about your services? What are some suggestions for making your program better?

Informal Telephone or "Point of Purchase" Surveys

Establish a form for staff and volunteers answering telephones to determine where the caller found the agency's phone number (i.e., yellow pages listing, public service announcement on radio, story in newspaper, word of mouth). Do the same if you have a box office, admissions area, or retail or thrift store.

Suggestion Box

Place a suggestion box in your facility with paper and pencils handy. Instruct your staff and volunteers to solicit suggestions from participants or visitors. Then read the suggestions and determine which ones are viable.

Attendance

Measure attendance at special events, classes, lectures, and meetings. If possible, ask those in attendance how they heard about the event.

All your evaluation techniques should be designed to determine which efforts are making the most impact. With limited resources, your agency needs to know how staff time and money are best spent to achieve maximum results.

Consider this scenario: You need volunteers. You and your staff spend twenty hours writing calendar notices, mailing them, and doing follow-up phone calls. You also produce five thousand flyers and find ways to distribute them—whew! As a result, you get five volunteers when you needed twenty. Through your networking with PR staff at other nonprofits, you learn that the Save the Snails Foundation just recruited twenty-five volunteers. How did they do that? Your counterpart at Save the Snails Foundation tells you he was able to convince his board to place a small ad in the Saturday "What To Do" section of the paper. For $600, the ad ran twice and the phones rang off the hook. The next time you need to recruit volunteers, maybe you can convince a major supporter to underwrite an ad (in addition to your normal recruitment efforts). Then ask new recruits what motivated them to volunteer. If you have three who read the calendar notice, one who responded to a flyer, and fifteen who saw the ad, you have solid information on where your resources should be spent.

There are other methods for evaluating what public relations activities will work for your organization. These methods depend on what kind of product or service you offer and what kinds of resources you have. For a cultural attraction dependent on admissions for revenue, a market survey will reveal a wealth of information about why people do or do not visit the facility.

Years ago, I worked for the local chapter of the American Red Cross, which also housed the regional blood bank. A market survey was done to determine why more people didn't donate blood. The answer was astonishingly simple: "Nobody asked me to give blood." That small piece of information dramatically altered the way the PR staff planned efforts for blood donor recruitment.

For an organization that supplies coats and blankets for homeless people, an evaluation technique may be as simple as working with police and shelters to observe the percentage of homeless people wearing coats and using blankets in an area where those items have been distributed. This can help determine if the donated items are actually being used by the recipients or if they are being sold or traded by the homeless for other goods.

The information presented in this chapter is offered to help you think about how to gather important data to help your nonprofit be more efficient and cost-effective. It is possible that "the way things have always been done" isn't the best approach. You might discover that a program or service your agency offers has become obsolete because of changing times or technology. For example, you don't see as many homes for unwed mothers today as you did thirty years ago, and job-training courses that don't offer classes on computer skills are not as effective as they need to be.

Use evaluation techniques to help your organization do its job better. You can save time, money, and frustration by knowing how effective your efforts are. You will also have good statistical data to use when you need to seek more staff or a larger budget for public relations activities at your agency. So starting right now, plug evaluation techniques into all PR plans and activities.

> Starting right now, plug evaluation techniques into all PR plans and activities.

Who Is on My Board of Directors and Why Should I Care?

·11·

A member of the local Save the Snails staff was obviously nervous and upset. She pulled constantly on a strand of hair, pursing her lips and muttering to herself as she paced in front of the copy machine. When asked what was wrong, she looked up, wide-eyed, and replied, "A board member is coming to the office to meet the staff." Her eyes reflected fear and her mouth quivered. She looked like she was going to cry.

Could a simple visit from a member of the board of directors upset a dedicated nonprofit agency staff person so much? Yes! Many staff see the board of directors as people on some elevated level of society who will surely breeze into the modest offices of the agency and make judgments on everything from how the office is decorated (or not decorated) to what staff are wearing or how neat their desks are. At most agencies, nothing could be further from the truth.

The board of directors of a nonprofit agency is the body that is empowered to make policy decisions, serve as the "boss" for the executive director, open doors in the community, and provide personal and professional financial assistance. They are usually people who care about the mission of the nonprofit and who serve on the board as volunteers because they genuinely want to help. In some cases, they are on the board because their boss told them to be or because it looks good on their resumé to serve on nonprofit boards, but more often than not, once they are in place, they buy into the agency and its mission and are tremendously supportive.

Makeup of the Board

A nominating or board development committee is usually responsible for recruiting new board members. In many organizations, key staff members are encouraged to make recommendations to the nominating committee. It is important to remember that the makeup of your board of directors can be the difference between maintaining the status quo and moving the agency forward.

There are certain categories of people who need to be on a nonprofit organization's board. They include as many top decision-makers from the community as your agency can recruit, from the CEO of the local telephone company to a bank president to the general manager of a TV station to the publisher of a newspaper. Having individuals on the board who are well connected in the community and personally committed to the mission of the nonprofit organization is vital. It is even better if these people are connected to your nonprofit's mission in some way, i.e., their children attend your after-school program, they used to be Scouts, they were in theater productions in college. Be careful, though. Don't go overboard. A board of directors for a fatal childhood disease that is made up only of parents of children with that malady can make for some emotional board meetings and some decisions that may be based more on personal concerns than agency needs.

- It is important that agency staff and the board chair put together an information packet for prospective board members that details the responsibilities and expectations of board participation.
- If your board meets four times a year, make it clear that attendance at those meetings is expected.
- If each board member is asked to be responsible for raising a certain amount of money each fiscal year, make that clear before someone agrees to serve on the board.
- If committee assignments are required, make sure that is in the board member's job description.
- Your organization should also consult its legal representative for information on liabilities board members might face from any lawsuits that could conceivably be filed against the nonprofit agency.

Policies should also be put into place that address how your agency deals with board members who agree to serve but simply do not participate in any way. Do you just wait out the end of their term or should your organization have a policy that tactfully dismisses a nonproductive board member in order to recruit someone else who is able to function more effectively? This is an issue that arises at some point for most organizations. It is a good idea to have in place a set policy for dealing with a nonproductive board member so that each member of the board is being as supportive of the organization as possible.

There are certain categories of people who need to be on a nonprofit organization's board.

In most agencies, members of the board of directors interface most often with the executive director, the staff person in charge of development (fundraising), and the public relations staff person. Boards usually consist of a chair (or president or chairman), co-chair, treasurer, secretary, and members who rotate on and off the board in terms ranging from one to three years. The officers of the board usually comprise the executive committee, which meets more often than the entire board and has the authority to make certain decisions without the consent of the full board of directors. Committees help make tasks more manageable by creating smaller segments of responsibility for projects.

What the Board Does

Most boards have a committee that deals with the public relations, communications, or marketing efforts for the nonprofit agency. The chair of that committee is the person you will deal with on a regular basis. I have had committee chairs who just showed up at board meetings and simply read a report that was written for them. I have had other chairpersons who have been totally hands-on in assisting and augmenting the communications efforts of the agency.

A board public relations committee chairperson can be a valuable asset, but you must be careful not to ask too much, rely too heavily on his or her help, or take that person for granted. You do not want to burn out, alienate, or irritate your committee chair. You do want practical advice, suggestions, and contacts from your committee. Your responsibility, however, is to make sure your committee chair knows the reality of what staff and budget resources the agency has—and doesn't have.

I worked with one organization where a board member was appalled that there was no website. He suggested that a committee of staff members be formed to plan for the launch of a site. Knowing that the agency didn't have the resources to make a website happen, we nonetheless formed a committee and requested that the board member attend the first few meetings. He quickly understood the reality that not only was the staff already overburdened with work, but there was absolutely no money to hire the help required to construct a website.

Using his contacts in the community, this board member found a webmaster willing to donate services and a volunteer to help the agency graphics person design the site. When the webpage was launched a few months later, it made a tremendous difference for the agency—a difference made specifically through the assistance of a member of the board of directors, who, when faced with the stark reality of limited resources, did something constructive to help.

I served on the board of directors for a small, child-serving agency and eagerly volunteered for the communications committee. The committee met monthly and was asked to be intensely hands-on with the annual report, press releases, media plans, and other very specific tasks normally handled by a staff person. Since there was no staff person at the time to tackle public relations efforts for the agency, the committee was being used to fulfill that function. Trying to handle those intense volunteer duties (along with the usual fundraising tasks assigned to all board members) and give my demanding, full-time job the attention it needed was too much. I had to resign from the committee and eventually also resigned from the board. They burned me out.

On the other side of the coin, as the PR and marketing staff person at a science museum, I had an outstanding chairperson who decided to expand the committee beyond board members. We recruited marketing and public relations professionals from the local convention center, a media-training agency, a major furniture store, public relations firms, a radio station, and a representative from city government. The resources that committee brought to the table were incredible!

My chair was careful to work with me to have focused projects that could be broken up into manageable small tasks so that no one committee member felt overwhelmed by a request for help. She also made sure that at each full board of directors meeting, she had a list of two or three things individual board members could do to help. These included suggesting companies who might become coupon partners, encouraging the board members to hold their own company holiday party at the museum to help the facility leasing department meet its revenue goal, and placing inserts about an upcoming exhibit in their companies' monthly bill.

The results of this chairperson's efforts were amazing—not only in widening the museum's PR/marketing efforts, but also in keeping communication issues front and center with the full board of directors.

Because your board of directors will most likely be tasked with setting financial policy and assisting with major fundraising initiatives as a primary function, the development (or fundraising) committee is essential. Public relations and fundraising always work closely together, so you will no doubt be involved with your board's development committee along with the executive director and any other staff who are responsible for fundraising.

Obviously, the fiscal health of a nonprofit is of utmost importance if the organization is going to achieve its mission and continue to grow in changing economic times. It takes resources to bring modern comput-

The fiscal health of a nonprofit is of utmost importance if the organization is going to continue to grow.

ers into a nonprofit organization, to train staff, and to pay escalating rent and salaries. Your board of directors can address issues surrounding fundraising with the benefit of knowing the current philanthropic philosophies within the business community. More and more, corporate givers want public relations or marketing benefits from their donations. The board can help assess this issue and work with you to understand how to help your fundraising staff craft win-win sponsorship proposals that include public relations and publicity components.

The Similar Syndromes Foundation board of directors is composed of twenty-one members. It meets quarterly, with executive committee meetings of the officers scheduled between each full board meeting. Its committee structure is as follows:

Executive Committee
    Chair, Co-chair, Secretary, Treasurer, and Executive Director of S.S.F.

Development Committee
    • Bank president, Chair
    • Owner of the local cable company
    • Principal in an accounting firm
    • CEO of the gas company

Public Relations Committee
    • PR agency senior account executive, Chair
    • PR director of a sports team
    • Community relations director of a computer company
    • CEO of a local dairy

Nominating Committee
    • Local lawyer, Chair
    • Vice president of an auto dealership
    • City council member
    • Physician who treats S.S.F. patients

Education Committee
    • School district supervisor, Chair
    • Manager of a retail chain regional office
    • High-tech company senior staff member
    • Telephone company executive

Consider using prominent retirees for the board. These individuals usually have a wealth of knowledge and contacts in the community and plenty of time to serve. (Just be careful not to choose someone with too much time who decides to become more involved in implementing policy rather than setting policy.)

Dealing with your agency's board of directors shouldn't be unnerving or frightening. Here are some practical tips:

- Never forget that these individuals are volunteers. Don't ask board members to tackle impossible tasks.
- Always remember that board members have real jobs, which must be their top priority.
- Unless a staff issue threatens the financial well-being of your agency, keep it to yourself. Board members do not want to hear staff members complain that they aren't paid enough, don't get enough vacation, or think Suzy Smith is incompetent.
- Don't ask for personal favors.
- Never distribute board members' addresses and private office phone numbers to the media or anyone else without permission.
- Respond promptly to requests.
- Ask the executive director, the development staff person, and the administrative person responsible for setting up board meetings for specific information that will help you work with the board.

Being able to work effectively with members of your board of directors is an important part of your job as a public relations professional. Board relations needn't be difficult, but an understanding of both your role and the role of the members of the board is essential. Different organizations have different atmospheres surrounding their boards, which you must investigate and understand.

On the whole, nonprofit organization board of directors members are dedicated people who care and want to use their expertise and contacts to help. Be appreciative, respectful, and responsive to your agency's board members, but don't be afraid of them.

■ Be appreciative, respectful, and responsive to your agency's board members, but don't be afraid of them.

What Do I Do in a Crisis Situation?

·12·

A few years ago, the artistic director of a children's performing theater decided to participate in a local arts festival with an adult puppet show he wrote and produced. This artist was extremely talented and eager to stretch his creative ability into a new arena, because the United States is the only country in the world that relegates puppetry to children. The show won critical acclaim and was performed without incident, until . . . At one performance a church minister wandered into the tent for the show. He noticed that a couple of mischievous children had sneaked under the tent flap at just about the time two puppets were engaging in what could have been construed as explicit sexual behavior. Afterwards, the minister was talking to a companion about the situation, lamenting the fact that the children had sneaked into the tent to view what he believed was inappropriate for them. As fate would have it, a reporter from the daily newspaper happened to be standing within earshot. You can imagine what happened next.

When the story appeared in the paper the next day, I contacted the theater's director, who was a good friend, and suggested he "batten down the hatches" and prepare for careful crisis communication. The artist was participating in the festival as a private individual, but because he was so associated with the theater, its name became totally entwined in the story. We quickly formulated a plan—which helped—but before it was over, the incident was discussed in depth on local talk radio and ended up as a joke on the *Tonight Show*! Fortunately, because of crisis communication efforts with the theater's board of directors and patrons, there were no lasting negative effects, such as reduced funding or a decrease in attendance.

This is a good example of why every nonprofit organization needs a crisis communication plan. And it is not enough to just prepare a plan; it must also be explained to all board members, volunteers, and staff, and it has to be updated and reinforced on a regular basis.

What is a crisis?
- Natural disaster: fire, tornado, hurricane, snowstorm, flood, mudslide
- Criminal act: robbery, bomb threat, shooting, hostage situation, protesters/picketers
- Internet crisis: damaging rumors in chat rooms, disgruntled former employees altering the agency website, hackers changing posted information
- Internal situations: accusations of wrongdoing by staff/volunteers, inappropriate/irresponsible behavior with clients, lawsuit by unhappy or "wronged" client

In an ideal world, there would never be a need to respond to negative situations, mistakes made by staff or volunteers, or natural disasters. Unfortunately, we don't live in an ideal world. What if a disgruntled ex-husband storms into a children's museum with a gun and takes hostages to call attention to his dispute with his ex-wife over child support? What if a worker at a nonprofit after-school program molests a child? How do you respond if the financial director of your agency has stolen money from donations? You never know what will happen that could garner negative publicity. Learn to expect the unexpected and be ready if a crisis occurs.

> Learn to expect the unexpected and be ready if a crisis occurs.

Creating a crisis communication plan is not difficult if you remember certain key elements. First, get help if you feel uncomfortable planning crisis communication.
- Contact someone at your national organization (if you have that kind of resource) and find out if there is a sample plan available.
- Ask for help from someone on your board of directors whose company has a plan.
- Form a committee of key staff people to brainstorm. Research plans from other organizations.
- A local public relations firm might be willing to donate some time to help you write a plan.

Choose a good spokesperson.
- You may want to choose the president of the board of directors and your executive director to be the crisis team spokespeople.
- You, as the public relations professional, can serve as the spokesperson internally for staff and volunteers.
- If your agency is fortunate enough to have a supportive local

celebrity, such as a sports figure, actor, or community philanthropist, ask that individual to assist.

Make sure everyone has the information he or she needs.
- Have a list of board and staff phone numbers both at the office and at home.
- Make sure media contact lists are accessible away from the office by someone other than the PR person in case that staff member is out of town or is incapacitated.
- Be sure to back up important computer information (financial records, volunteer lists, donor information) at least weekly and keep copies of backup disks in a safe deposit box or other secure place. Remember, if the crisis concerns a disaster (such as a fire in your building, a major crippling storm, or a hostile individual taking over the office) you must have critical information secured in a safe place off site.

Be proactive, honest, and positive in your crisis communication.
- Get all of the facts surrounding the situation.
- With your crisis team, evaluate exactly what happened and discuss what the impact might be on the general public, your staff, volunteers, donors, and other supporters.
- Always tell the truth. Sometimes it is difficult to admit that someone involved with your agency has made a mistake, but the truth is far better than trying to cover up the facts.
- Determine your message. Think about questions the media might ask and decide how best to respond.
- Try to phrase your comments so they reflect what's best for the public rather than focusing on what's best for your agency.
- Take a positive tack with any situation. If someone embezzled money, communicate that the agency is pleased to have discovered the situation before any more damage was done and praise the individual or system that enabled discovery of the crime. If a volunteer has done something inappropriate, note that the agency tries to make sure all its volunteers are screened carefully, but mistakes happen and the agency is glad this is the only time in its fifty-year history that this has occurred. Assure the public that the agency will evaluate screening programs to make sure they are as thorough as possible. The media and the public appreciate honest and timely responses to crisis situations.

Follow up and evaluate.
- Be sure to have an evaluation session to determine the effectiveness of your response to the crisis situation. Were there parts of the plan that didn't work well? Did you forget a critical piece, like a backup in case your spokesperson was out of town or ill?
- Always follow up after the fact on anything you or your spokespersons have indicated would be done differently in the event of another crisis situation.
- If you stated that the agency would change its policy in some way, send out a media advisory when that has been accomplished, noting how well it works.
- Learn from a crisis so that if something happens again it can be handled more smoothly.

No one likes to think of negative situations, but having a crisis communication plan is a little like taking an umbrella in case of rain. In my experience, when I actually remember to carry my umbrella, it usually doesn't rain.

Sample Crisis Communications Plan

If needed, separate policies can be developed for specific situations. For example, a bomb threat at a cultural attraction (like an art museum that has a Monet exhibition in place) must be handled differently from a bomb threat in an office building in which your agency rents space. Social service organizations that deal with clients should have a policy in place for detailed documentation of services—such as whether female counselors meet privately with male clients—to be available in the event of a lawsuit by a disgruntled person.

Who is on the crisis team?
- Executive director – Serves as chief spokesperson
- Board president – Is contacted by executive director if needed or by other staff if executive director is not available
- Public relations staff person – Deals with media and serves as official spokesperson if executive director and board president are not available
- Fundraising or education staff – Assists with media and serves as crisis manager
- Financial staff – Provides necessary financial data
- Building services personnel – If the nonprofit organization owns the facility or is responsible for it (such as a zoo, museum, client

counseling center, theater, or substance abuse hospital), it is especially important to have building services staff involved
- Agency's legal representative and auditors – Advises legal rights and responsibilities and appropriate action to take
- Other staff as needed

*Note: Be sure all staff know the team structure and refer **all** inquiries to the proper people to avoid dissemination of misinformation.*

What does the crisis team do?
- Plans strategy and acts immediately if a crisis situation occurs
- Identifies organizational spokespersons, provides them with media training, and goes over every aspect of the crisis plan once it is completed
- Creates a contact list for each person on the crisis team.

Note: List spokespersons in the order they should be contacted, and post this information in all offices. Make sure everyone has a copy of the names and titles of the spokespersons with all their telephone numbers—home, office, cell phone, car phone, and pager. Everyone on the team should keep this information both in the office and at home.

Think about staging a mock crisis event to test your plan.

First Steps
1. Before any crisis occurs, the team should brainstorm about what kinds of situations could possibly happen to your agency.
   - Discuss ways to handle those scenarios.
   - Designate a place for the crisis team to meet—in the organization's office, in someone's home, or at the board president's office.
   - Set aside a crisis management budget.
2. The chief spokesperson and media liaison person must meet (if only by phone) as soon as possible after an incident to determine what the reality of the situation is and what will be said immediately—both to the staff and to the media.
3. It is all right to tell the media that you will get back to them in a timely manner after you assess the situation.
   - Don't feel forced to speak before you have all the facts.
   - Don't let the media intimidate you by saying they are "on deadline." In a crisis situation they can stretch deadlines.

- Immediately meet with staff and volunteers (if appropriate) to discuss the situation.
- Determine if anyone else has additional information about the crisis.
- Reiterate the importance of referring all questions to key members of the crisis team.
- Emphasize that the goal is to avoid inaccurate information being given to the media and thus to the public.
4. When dealing with the media be sure to:
   - Tell the truth.
   - Respond to all questions, even if the response is that you will get back to them.
   - Don't respond to hypothetical questions (e.g., What if the gunman is a staff member?).
   - Remember that nothing is ever "off the record."
   - Never volunteer negative information.
   - Stay calm. Don't lose your temper.
5. Be sure that all staff members know what their role is in handling the situation. Answer their questions as thoroughly as possible.

Taking Action

1 Assess your physical surroundings.
   - Is the power out?
   - Does the crisis team need to move to another location for access to computers and telephones?
   - Did the incident involve someone associated with the organization in another location, such as at a meeting site or in a training facility?
   - Are staff and volunteers in any danger?
   - Take any action necessary to ensure safety and to be able to deal with the situation.
2 Once internal necessities have been handled, the crisis team should convene to discuss the message that will be communicated in response to inquiries from the media and any other callers.
3. Determine if the agency needs to interface with local authorities. If so, appoint a staff member to handle that duty.
4. As soon as that message is confirmed, a press release or media advisory should be drafted and provided to staff and media.
5. Depending upon the magnitude of the situation, decide if a

press conference is needed. If so,
- Arrange one quickly.
- Call the media to let them know when and where it will take place.
- Assemble key players.
- Provide written statements for spokespersons to read.

6. Decide if there is any need for psychological counseling for staff, clients, or the public because of the crisis situation.

Follow-Up

1. Once the immediate situation has been evaluated and dealt with and the media has been briefed, there is a period of time when periodic follow-up with the media may be needed. If there is a child missing from one of your agency's programs, release periodic statements to the press about efforts to find the child. If there are protesters or a bomb threat, communicate progress in negotiations.
2. Make and post signs advising that the building is closed and/or listing an alternative phone number to call for assistance.
3. Assign staff to off-site locations to offer assistance if necessary.
4. During this period, the entire crisis team will need to stay in close touch and be of one voice in what is communicated to the media and thus to the public.
5. Continue in the follow-up phase as long as needed.

Evaluation

1. Once the crisis is resolved, the agency should return to normal operation as soon as possible.
2. The crisis team spokesperson should declare the emergency over. Using the media liaison staff person:
   - Disseminate a press release.
   - Put the information on phone voice mail.
   - Send a letter to the editor of the newspaper thanking people for their support.
   - Reassure staff.
   - Mail a letter to clients, donors, and agency members, if appropriate.
3. Hold a debriefing session with the crisis team to discuss questions, concerns, or perceived mistakes during the emergency.

Here are some fictional scenarios with sample messages:

A major snowstorm causes the collapse of the roof of a building where a credit counseling class is being held. Three students are injured.

> The Credit Counseling Service sponsoring the classes responds that it is always concerned for the safety of its clients. The building used for the classes was structurally sound but had never experienced the amount of wet, heavy snow that fell in this freak storm. The agency will explore the necessity of canceling classes in the future in the event of a major storm or natural phenomenon of any kind. Further, the agency is investigating what insurance it and the building management have that will help cover medical costs for those injured.

An eccentric pseudoscientist claims that megadoses of a certain mineral will cure a disease. Families of patients mount a vocal, public campaign to know why the agency that funds patient assistance and research for the specific disease is not supporting the claim.

> The XYZ Foundation assures its members and the general public that it investigates any and all claims of therapies that will help patients with XYZ disease. The organization's primary concern is for the health and safety of patients. While the foundation understands the deep concern of patients and their families, it would be irresponsible to endorse megadoses of any substance—pharmaceutical or natural herbal supplement—without careful research into possible negative side effects. The foundation points to current research that is looking into new drug therapies that will be fully tested to ensure they will help XYZ patients. The public is encouraged to visit the foundation's website for detailed information about XYZ disease and the research efforts being done to find better treatment and, ultimately, a cure.

Remember that honest, timely responses and a careful investigation of the facts are vital in handling any emergency situation. And you should also broaden your thinking about what constitutes a crisis. For instance:

■ Honest, timely responses and a careful investigation of the facts are vital in handling any emergency situation.

The boys choir from a major city took its traveling choir to Italy for its annual overseas concert tour. There were two Jewish boys in the choir whose families had arranged with friends in Italy for the boys to go to their home for a Friday evening seder. In Italy, the choir director refused to let the boys go separately from the rest of the choir to the Italian home. The parents were very upset and contacted the local newspaper and radio stations. A part of their ire was that the choir was singing part of the Easter celebration at the Vatican and they felt their Jewish children were being discriminated against. It became a huge controversy in the choir's hometown. If the choir director had made it clear before the trip that no boys would be allowed separate trips while in Italy because he had been advised by the U.S. State Department that American children were often targeted for terrorist attacks in Italy at that time, the situation might not have reached the level of frenzy it did.

Remember the part of your crisis communication plan that advises you to anticipate problems or reactions? Here is an excellent example:

A museum whose major audience is children brought in a traveling exhibit from Greece that explored the origins and past one hundred years of the Olympics. Within the exhibit were wonderful reproductions of classic Greek statues—nude, of course. They came with the exhibit and were an integral part of it. The museum posted a sign at the entrance to the exhibit warning parents that there were nude statues. Parents who didn't want their children to see the statues didn't enter the exhibit area. There was only one complaint to the museum about the nudity. In fact, the worst thing that happened was a child swung on the outstretched arm of the chariot master statue, causing it to break off. Fortunately, it was a reproduction, and Super Glue is a wonderful thing.

Don't expect a crisis, but do be prepared for any kind of emergency situation you can imagine. I hope your crisis communication plan will work like my umbrella: once you have the plan in place, you won't need it.

Why Should I Push for an Advertising Budget?

·13·

It's time for nonprofits to rethink their philosophy on paid advertising. Sticking your toes into the world of advertising doesn't mean that you will use it to replace all other forms of communication. It only means that you will broaden your horizons and have the advantage of controlling your message and the placement of that message. Advertising doesn't even have to totally replace public service announcements (PSAs), but as discussed in Chapter 4, Why Must I Have Media Relations?, the days of getting your local television station to tape a sixty-second PSA to air for free are mostly gone. When the Federal Communication Commission deregulated public service time, things began to change.

The Demise of PSAs As They Used to Be

In the old days, television stations were required to air a certain number of PSAs each month. As the public service director at a CBS affiliate, a large part of my job was to screen PSAs sent to the station and then fill them in on the daily station log. The station's license renewal depended (in part) on keeping that commitment. When the PSA requirement was no longer in place, most stations continued their support for nonprofits in their viewing area by providing voluntary public service time. Over the years, as cable stations have increased and the war of the ratings at local stations has heated up, available public service time has dwindled.

Yes, there is still television public service time available, but it is more likely to be a shared station identification at the top of the hour, where your agency's logo appears with the station's call letters for five seconds. Community calendar listings are popular on morning news programs that run from five or six in the morning until network news shows start at 7:00 A.M. Some stations still do air fifteen- or thirty-second taped PSAs, but those are rare and usually in smaller markets. Networks will also use PSAs to fill time when advertising is not sold, but those spots have to have national appeal and are often provided by the National Advertising Council.

Your agency should continue to seek free time on radio and television and free space in the local paper. It is also important, however, to do your homework and find out what the station's public service/public affairs philosophy is. I know of one station that for a period of time would not use any PSA that asked its viewers to provide financial support for a nonprofit. That station's philosophy was that any PSA it aired must inform its viewers and provide useful information. That's when you get creative—the humane society could offer tips for parents on how to avoid dog bites and the local child abuse council could provide lists of ways to keep your child safe in a shopping mall.

A simple phone call or meeting with the person tasked with handling public service at the radio, television station, or newspaper will provide you with the information you need to make the most effective use of what public service time is available. Sometimes the media will even have written guidelines for public service.

Many stations have blended what used to be public service with public affairs and now rely more on a community relations program, where the station gets more involved in the community by using its access to the public to address certain urgent problems—like violence, homelessness, traffic congestion, pollution, or disaster relief. You should use public service, community relations, or public affairs (or whatever local stations call their donated community service time) whenever possible, but to rely on PSAs as your organization's sole avenue for informing people about needs and activities is shortsighted. In today's world, you can both advertise and take advantage of PSAs. It used to be that if a nonprofit organization used paid advertising in the newspaper, a radio station might not give the agency public service. That isn't true anymore.

> To rely on PSAs as your organization's sole avenue for informing people about needs and activities is shortsighted.

Include Advertising in Your Nonprofit Organization Budget

Advertising isn't a dirty word for nonprofit organizations. If you think about it, PSAs are also advertising (with the disadvantage of not having any control of your message or when the spots run). With the information super highway rolling along, the public is bombarded with messages from all sides, all the time. A few PSAs are not going to get through that kind of noise. To really make a difference and give your agency a leg up, you should consider advertising as part of a coordinated campaign: PR, marketing, and advertising.

You know, I can hear you laughing and muttering something like, "Yeah, like my executive director and board are going to budget money for advertising—when hell freezes over they will!"

Wrong attitude. You must convince your agency that this is the way to go. We know that advertising works. Otherwise, those irritating car salesmen wouldn't be screaming at us on TV in reverberation about how low their prices are. If advertising didn't work, why would national companies pay enormous prices for thirty-second advertisements during the broadcast of the World Series or Super Bowl? Take it as a given that advertising is going to help your agency better attain its goals. Then, investigate and gather facts:

1. If there is another nonprofit in your area that has tried paid advertising, see if any members will share information with you on the results of their efforts. They probably won't wish to divulge financial details but may be willing to tell you in general how their advertising campaign worked for them.

2. Check with the local advertising council or advertising club for statistics about the effectiveness of advertising.

3. Arm yourself with figures. Find out the advertising rates for radio, TV, and print media. Ask if ad salespeople will work with nonprofits by offering discounts or providing value-added incentives.

4. List all the different opportunities for advertising. Look at who your agency's target audience is and find avenues to reach them. Don't forget small periodicals, neighborhood association newsletters, the Internet, billboards, public radio stations, school publications, or signs on taxies/buses and marquees.

5. Find out if a radio station is willing to give your organization some free airtime as a trade-out for tickets to an event you sponsor that the station can use as on-air giveaways.

Once you start delving into the possibilities for low-cost, effective advertising, you will be amazed at how far you can stretch a teeny-tiny advertising budget of, say, $5,000. I am not qualified to give you a quick overview of "Advertising 101." What I can do is provide you with thoughts and ideas about what I have seen work for some nonprofits.

■ You should consider advertising as part of a coordinated campaign that also includes PR and marketing.

Let's Plan an Ad Campaign

Who, What, When, Where?

Let's take your $5,000 and start to plan what you want to promote, during what time period, and to what audience. I am going to assume you represent a small, countywide humane society. Through public relations efforts, you have already hooked up with a pet store to hold off-site adoption days, free flea baths, or rabies shots. Once a week, the local TV station lets you bring an animal on its morning show to highlight for adoption. Things are going fairly well, but Easter is coming up and you know that a few weeks later your shelter will be flooded with animals that were purchased as holiday presents for kids. It just didn't work out for the family when the adorable, fluffy little chicks and ducklings became full-grown chickens and ducks. Instead of worrying about what to do with all those animals, you are proposing to your executive director and board that the organization try an advertising campaign to see if you can prevent the problem from occurring in the first place.

Carefully planning ahead, you are able to place ads in four neighborhood association quarterly newsletters at a cost of from $75 to $110. These ads are placed in the spring issue, which is delivered to homes from late February to mid-March. You sent your advertising copy to the newsletter editors in January. Your total cost is $375.

The local Public Broadcasting Station (PBS) offers nonprofits something called "scheduled broadcast announcements" or "sponsorships," which are a cross between PSAs and regular paid advertising (which most PBS stations do not do). The benefit is that these announcements are scheduled to run at a specific time. There may be guidelines, however, on what you can say in these announcements. Since the station has to raise its own funds, you might not be allowed to run any spot that solicits donations. But that isn't a concern here since you are trying to get people to think carefully before purchasing live animals as gifts at Easter. At $85 each, four of these spots placed two weeks before Easter cost $340.

A monthly parenting magazine for your region of the state will run a quarter-page ad for $420 in its March issue. As added value, they will also write an article about the issue of giving live animals to children and will refer readers with questions to your agency. The magazine reaches fifty-five thousand households of involved, concerned parents.

The "oldies" radio station, which you know most grandparents and many parents enjoy, will give you a schedule of ten thirty-second advertising spots over a two-day period and will have their morning DJs give away free spaying and neutering coupons to the first three people who adopt a pet from your shelter. The cost for this is $2,000.

An outdoor advertising company allows nonprofits to use empty billboard space free of charge. The agency has to have the posters printed to install on the board or pay to have the board painted, whichever method is used by that particular company. You can't choose the location of the billboards, but this is still a good opportunity. Using printed posters as our example, we find that it will cost $800 to print two posters and $200 to have them installed.

Production Costs

You have now spent $4,135. The remaining money should be reserved for costs associated with producing the ads for the space you have decided to purchase. Those costs could include:
- Paying a graphic designer
- Having the ad design converted to film or disk for the printer to use
- Paying for audio tape for radio spots

Note: These figures are estimates. Actual costs vary in different communities and generally go up every year.

What's the Message?

You have decided where you want to place your advertising and now you must determine what your message will be and who will write that message. You have several choices:
- Determine what you think is the right message and write the ads yourself
- Brainstorm with other staff or get your board PR committee to help
- If you work with an advertising agency, ask for their help
- Pay a freelancer to write your ads

For your first advertising effort, you may want to consider deciding on the concept and the message in conjunction with other staff. If you have a board member in the communication or advertising field, seek his or her counsel. The most important thing to remember when creating ads is that you have very limited time to capture someone's attention. A billboard allows just four to eight seconds to grab attention as people whiz down the road. A thirty-second radio spot is pretty short. The message needs to be concise, clever, and memorable. Print ads must be clean, with a tag line and graphic that will stand out from other ads on the page. Keep your message short, to the point, and interesting.

For the humane society campaign, it might be effective for the print ads and billboards to show pictures of a baby chick and an adult chicken or rooster with the message:

"This [picture of baby chick] becomes this [picture of adult chicken]. Think before you buy chicks this spring. They are a growing responsibility."

Place your agency name and phone number (big enough to read) underneath the message.

Creating the Ad

The next consideration is how to physically create the ad. If you have a graphics design person on staff, he or she can produce the ad on the computer. If you outsource your newsletter, annual report, or brochures, you can pay the person who does that work for the agency to create your ads. That's why we saved some money out of the $5,000 budget—to pay for these kinds of production costs.

Radio copy is easier because you can simply write it and an announcer at the station will record it for you. In the best of all worlds, you would hire an actor and produce your radio ad in the studio with great sound effects. But that is very expensive. (Sometimes the "talent" will donate his or her skills or do the work at the minimum scale allowed by the union.)

Your radio script may read like this:

"Easter is coming and many people are tempted to purchase baby chicks and ducklings as presents for their kids. Think before you do. These adorable living creatures will grow up to be adult chickens and ducks. If you won't be able to care for them when they are grown, don't buy them now. This message is sponsored by the XYZ Humane Society. 999-888-7777."

The effectiveness of this small advertising campaign can be evaluated by looking at the numbers of unwanted chickens and ducks turned over to the shelter. If that number is substantially down from previous years, you know your advertising worked! You can also evaluate the money saved by not having to house, adopt out, or otherwise place or euthanize the unwanted pets. Be sure to factor in staff time and overhead costs. Compare these figures to the money spent on the advertising effort. You might find that you spent less money to advertise than the organization would have spent having to deal with large numbers of unwanted animals.

A Look at *Pro Bono* Advertising

I think it is important to take a moment to talk about *pro bono* (without compensation, for the public good) advertising. A wonderful advertising agency with an outstanding reputation represented a museum as a *pro bono* client. The agency produced copy and graphics for the limited number of ads the museum was able to buy. When an exhibition about the human body came to the museum, agency people visited the exhibit to find out what components were in the displays. They seemed particularly taken with a video autopsy that was visually transmitted onto a human form. When the concept for the ad was submitted to the museum, it read "Oh, no, not another bloody glove!" (Understand that this was in the middle of the O. J. Simpson trial, and a bloody glove had just been introduced into evidence.) The advertising agency thought the copy was clever and avant-garde. The museum thought it was totally inappropriate for the family audience it sought to attract. It was the nonprofit's public relations person who had to channel the advertising agency's desire to be creative and different in a direction that would satisfy their needs *and* be effective for the museum.

You can see that having advertising professionals adopt your organization free of charge can be a wonderful advantage but offers unique challenges as well. Since you, as the public relations person, will probably be the one to interface with an agency account representative, remember these points so you will have a mutually satisfying relationship:

1. Understand exactly how long the relationship will last: one year? five years? Be aware of why the advertising agency wants to represent your organization as a *pro bono* client. Usually, the ad agency staff are allowed to be a little more creative with a *pro bono* account and can stretch their talents to create interesting materials that can be entered into competition for prestigious advertising awards. Sometimes, however, they tend to forget that the nonprofit organization, albeit *pro bono*, is still a "client."

2. Be sure you both understand what "out-of-pocket" expenses the nonprofit agency will be responsible for covering. Will your organization be billed for every copy made, faxes, computer input, mileage, creative time, or production costs? Are those expenses being billed at the advertising agency's cost or at the rate they normally bill their corporate clients?

3. Establish a relationship that promotes good communication. Nothing is worse than trying to work with an advertising agency whose employees treat you and your staff like you know absolutely nothing about who your audience is or what message

you want or need to communicate. Conversely, your staff must understand and appreciate the expertise of the advertising agency personnel and listen to their recommendations.

4. Remember that you are a *pro bono* client and the ad agency's paying clients will come first in a tight deadline situation. Build in plenty of time for projects to cover situations where your job must be pushed back on the schedule.

5. Never forget that the ad agency is doing you a service and that its employees who work on your materials are basically volunteers. Be courteous, respectful of their time, and generous in both public and private thank-yous for their efforts.

With or without a professional ad agency to assist, advertising can be a tremendous benefit for nonprofits. Your task is to do your homework, start slowly, don't be afraid to ask for advice, and remember to evaluate the effectiveness of any advertising efforts. Once you have been able to demonstrate the value of this tool to your executive director and board, push to have an advertising line item included in your yearly expense budget.

Who Are My Volunteers?

·14·

Volunteer positions at nonprofit organizations can be as varied as are the people who fill those jobs. Your volunteers may be board members, museum docents, celebrity spokespeople, envelope-stuffers, fundraising gala committee members, thrift shop cashiers, or drivers. Almost all nonprofits depend on volunteers to help further their agency's mission in a cost-effective way. It is essential for you, the public relations person, to understand what motivates volunteers and to make sure the entire agency staff also understands and knows how to treat volunteers appropriately.

There are many things that compel people to become volunteers. I know one very busy man (running three businesses) who became a Big Brother because he wanted to give something back for all of his blessings. A celebrity decided to lend his name to the Alzheimer's Association because his mother suffered from the disease. Another famous person worked with Toys for Tots because her publicist told her to do it. A board member for a large, national nonprofit participates because it looks good on his resumé. An elderly, disabled woman, retired from years of work as a cleaning lady, volunteers at her grandson's school, partly because she always wanted to be a teacher but mostly because working with children really makes her feel good.

Regardless of their motives, volunteers give freely of their time and talent to help nonprofit organizations by doing a variety of jobs. As the public relations person, your task is to make sure all of the volunteers feel appreciated, recognized, and properly thanked. Working closely with the staff person responsible for recruiting and training volunteers, make an effort to meet the volunteers in order to find out things about them that might be of interest to the staff or the media.

Establishing a good relationship between paid staff and volunteers

Establishing a good relationship between paid staff and volunteers is very important.

■

is very important. From your PR perspective, always think about volunteers when preparing press releases or arranging for radio or TV coverage. If you are writing about the completion of a successful fundraising campaign, quote the chair of your board of directors, who should attribute reaching that goal to the campaign volunteers. Schedule a photo shoot of the committee members for use in the print media—and please have the volunteers doing something interesting. Get them to hold up paper dollar signs or have them hoist the campaign chairperson on their shoulders like a winning football coach. Your development staff person may have worked ten hours a day during the campaign—nagging, pleading, following up, and doing all the mailings—but in the publicity about the fundraising campaign, all credit and thanks go to the volunteers. The reality is that staff may work really hard, but that is their job. And the truth is that without the contacts and business ability of the fundraising volunteers, the staff simply could not have raised as much money. Don't ever forget that.

Maybe your agency delivers meals to AIDS patients. You have arranged for a television station to follow one volunteer during her rounds to see firsthand how the program works effectively because of the volunteers. Your agency's staff coordinator may agonize over schedules, change a tire for a volunteer, and actually deliver meals herself when a volunteer doesn't show up. Again, the reality is that without the volunteers, that agency would not be able to serve as many people. Focus publicity on what the volunteers do.

- Once a year, use the total number of volunteer hours and a "Volunteer of the Year" award to demonstrate how your organization values its volunteers.
- Television reporters love clever visuals. Think of a way to show how the donated volunteer hours help. Perhaps you can use a stack of play money to represent how many dollars were saved by not having to hire additional staff.
- For radio you need to create good sound bites: "It would have taken an additional staff member three years to accomplish what four volunteers did in six months. These good citizens should be wearing super-hero outfits with capes!" This serves the dual purpose of recognizing your wonderful volunteers' contributions and helping recruit future volunteers.

Beyond using media for publicity about your volunteer activities, there are other ways to recognize them and ensure that they feel valued and appreciated. Working in conjunction with the volunteer coordinator on your organization's staff, think about implementing some of the following programs for volunteer recognition:

1. Make sure volunteers have the opportunity to help with the "fun stuff."
   - If your agency has been selected to receive twenty free tickets to a home game of the city's major league baseball team, allocate five or ten of those tickets for volunteers to use.
   - If you need staffing assistance at the annual black tie fundraising event that benefits your nonprofit, be sure to offer volunteers the opportunity to help. Some of them may never have been able to attend such an event.
   - A celebrity has come forward to support your cause. Try to arrange a brief meeting with your volunteers, so they can meet the celebrity.
2. Include a volunteer spotlight column in the agency newsletter. In each issue of your newsletter, feature a different volunteer with a photograph and paragraph about that person.
3. Enter your agency's volunteers in citywide, state, or regional competitions. Keep your eyes and ears open and identify a volunteer who is truly outstanding to enter into these kinds of special recognition events. In one city, a local television station gives out community service awards each year. Ten local volunteers are selected and a video is made about them and their volunteer activities. These top volunteers are then honored at a lavish awards banquet that is televised locally in prime time. Entering a volunteer in this competition is a fairly labor-intensive chore, with a lot of paperwork, but it is well worth it to show appreciation for an outstanding volunteer and to put the spotlight on your organization. See if these or similar options are available in your community:
   - A major drugstore chain had a competition for the one hundred best community volunteers. A short essay and entry form were required.
   - Some city newspapers have "Volunteer of the Year" awards.
4. Hold quarterly, semi-annual, or annual volunteer appreciation parties. My elderly mother never misses a volunteer party at the local botanical garden, where she puts in four or five hours a week in the library. It is an opportunity for her to get dressed up, talk to other people, and feel very special. It really helps keep her going every week, even when she might not feel like volunteering. Refreshments and entertainment can be underwritten by a major agency sponsor, or, with careful planning, you can budget the expense for these parties each year as budgets are being built.
5. Have a "Volunteer of the Month" parking spot. Provide a special parking space close to the entrance to your building for the Volunteer

of the Month.

6. Recognize special occasions. Send birthday greetings or cards recognizing the anniversary of when someone started volunteering. If your agency staff is small enough, let everyone sign these cards.

Volunteers benefit public relations activities at every level of your organization. They are your goodwill ambassadors. They don't have to worry about budgets or annual reports, so they have more time to interact with your clients. Treat your volunteers with dignity and respect and they will be loyal, dedicated supporters for years.

I close the section on volunteers with a story about a favorite volunteer of mine. Carolyn followed me from one nonprofit to another, always willing to do whatever was needed. She liked to work one-day special events. In her tenure, she stapled noses on paper puppets for six hours for a never-ending stream of enthusiastic children, handed out stickers at an outdoor event in the freezing cold, demonstrated laws of physics by pulling a tablecloth out from under real, breakable dishes over and over again, and answered the same question ("Where's the bathroom?") about seven thousand times. Carolyn was a super volunteer, and she won my total appreciation and complete admiration one day at a family-oriented event on drug prevention. The local police brought a drug-sniffing dog for kids to meet. The dog had never been around so many hyper kids, who were running, jumping, petting him, and making funny faces. The poor dog got sick and threw up. Carolyn took complete charge, maneuvering the kids away, grabbing paper towels to clean up the mess, and comforting the dog. Now that's a volunteer!

Make sure your volunteers feel valued and appreciated. ■

Where Is My Website?

·15·

What do you mean you don't have a website? In this age of the Internet, it is imperative that every nonprofit organization that has a need to communicate with its public have a website.

- If you are an arts or cultural institution and need to direct traffic to your museum or theater, a website can create interest and compel people to visit. You can even book group visits and sell individual tickets on your site.
- If you are a church, a website is a thoroughly modern way to witness and minister to people who don't like "organized religion." Provide online prayer circles and accept prayer requests through your site.
- If you are a health care agency, a website can be an incredible educational tool. Post symptoms of a disease, list specialists in the field, and provide links to support groups and other related sites.
- If you are a humane society, post photographs of adorable animals (or, if you are more technologically sophisticated, use video) on your website. List places and dates for pet adoptions, animal health tips, locations for free flea dips, or facts about rabies.

This chapter is not a how-to on step-by-step website construction. You really need to consult an expert in that field because it is so important to do it right. I *can* tell you some of the things I believe make a website effective and provide you with ideas on how to get up and running without spending an arm and a leg.

If you plan to create your agency's website yourself, you will need to take specific courses, have an instructor, and/or purchase one of the many books and software programs on building websites. A better course of action may be to find a college student volunteer to help your nonprofit get on the Internet. Perhaps a college technology student can receive credit through an internship for helping you set up your site. I strongly recommend that you consult an expert, however, so your agency will be well represented in cyber space, because just as the look of your printed material is important (Chapter 6, Why Is the Look Important?), so is the look of your website.

There are many people and companies providing help for website development. Some Internet access services will help nonprofits establish a site. For a fee, web companies will create and manage your site, updating it periodically and making sure links are set up to other appropriate sites. This can be expensive, but in reviewing options, remember that creating a website is not a task for amateurs.

To get a better idea of how nonprofit organizations should approach web design companies, I contacted Dan Kehoe, whose Atlanta-based company, Getting You Online, provides many services for his clients, from designing the site to coding and programming (i.e., HTML, java script) to server maintenance and online promotions (submitting your site to search engines). Dan believes that in the future, nonprofit agencies will include services from web companies in their expense budgets as a necessary commodity, similar to phone service, voice mail systems, and fax machines. However, right now he advises that it is possible to find a web company willing to work with you *pro bono*. A large web company may include a certain percentage of charitable work in their strategic plans. Smaller companies may view the donation of their expertise to a nonprofit agency as an opportunity to market their services, especially if you can craft a win-win relationship that offers mutual benefits. For example:

> It is possible to get web design services for free. ■

- Devise a way to promote the web design company to your members through your newsletter or other regular mailings.
- Agree to acknowledge the web assistance donation in printed materials and on your web page.
- Prepare a press release about the donation and the web design company at the time your site is launched so both your site and their company receive good publicity.
- If your agency has an annual conference or convention, offer the web company a free booth at that meeting.
- Does your agency print T-shirts for supporters, staff, and volunteers? Why not put the web company's logo on those shirts?
- If appropriate, place signage in your facility: "Save the Snails appreciates the generous donation of services from Getting You Online."

However you decide to get your website up and running, careful consideration should be given to the design of the site and what information will be contained on it.

Know Your Audience

The first step is to know who your audience is and understand what your objectives are.

- If your audience is senior citizens, you may need to structure your web page so that it is accessed by middle-aged people who can then provide the information to their parents. While seniors are a growing market for computers, most are still not flocking to the Internet.
- If your audience is children, the design of the page will need to be structured with lots of primary colors and graphics.
- If the general public is your target, keep your information easy to read and stay away from difficult scientific terms or agency jargon that most people will not understand.

What is the Purpose of Your Site?

- Is it purely informational? Do you want it to serve as research information for people interested in the disease your agency works to cure?
- Do you want the site to motivate people to do something (visit your theater, become a volunteer for your organization, write a letter to their congressman)?
- Do you need to make your site interactive? Can visitors click on or link to more detailed information? Can they e-mail your agency with comments, questions, or suggestions? Will their e-mail be acknowledged in a timely way?

Eye-Catching Website Design

When deciding what to put on a website, remember that scanning a computer screen is different from reading a book. Like a billboard or a tabletop display, your website has a limited amount of time to catch people's interest and entice them to read on.

- Instead of posting your entire annual report on the site, consider just using highlights and invite people to contact the office to order a hard copy, or let them click on an icon to access the entire report.
- Try to edit information into concise paragraphs and use bullet points.

- Set up your site so that if visitors want more complete information about a topic, they can easily click for more details or contact your office immediately by e-mail.

Make Your Site Media-friendly

One of the biggest complaints media representatives have about websites is the lack of easily accessible contact information. Create a press shortcut on your home page so media can click and have immediate access to the person in your agency handling PR duties. List the person's name, title, street address, e-mail address, and phone, fax, and cell numbers.

A press page should also include links to agency press releases (current through the past few months). Media would also appreciate downloadable graphics—your logo, stock press photos, and pictures and bios of your top staff and board members.

Work with the person who designs the graphics for your site to make it as attractive and readable as possible. Remember that on your website, just as in printed publications, good design and white space make information easier to read. Also, discuss security issues, especially if you plan to solicit donations or purchases via credit card information. Can a disgruntled former employee, a hacker, or a volunteer access the site to post inappropriate information? You can't stop experienced hackers, but you can make it a lot harder for them. Encrypted systems help protect personal credit information.

Think about the ways you want to "reach out and touch" people through your presence on the Internet. Look at other organizations' websites to see what you like and what you find boring or ineffectual. It doesn't take long to see the difference between good sites and ineffective ones. Like other publications produced by your nonprofit, the website portrays an image about your agency. Don't create something boring, stuffy, inaccurate, or difficult to read. Above all, Dan Kehoe believes your site has to be compelling, because as a nonprofit you are seeking something from people with not much in return (volunteering, donating, taking some kind of action).

Dan also reminds you to understand how to size files. If you plan for a site that utilizes large files, it will take too long for visitors to load those files when they access your web page. Graphics are very important because they will enhance your site, but stay away from large photographs or too much animated art. While they may be very attractive, some visitors to your site may be irritated because the pictures take so long to download. Again, keep uppermost in your mind exactly what you are trying to accomplish with your website. Defining the purpose will help you decide what information to include.

Once your site is ready, you or someone on the staff at your organization can learn how to update written information. It isn't as easy as using word processing, but it isn't rocket science either. Your web company can help your staff learn this procedure. If you want to update simple text, like upcoming events, it is relatively easy to do. There are software programs that automatically convert text to HTML code. You may need some tips on HTML so you are able to correct any glitches in the software. And you will probably need another software program (which can usually be obtained for free) to upload agency updates onto your website.

It sounds intimidating, but like any other new skill, it is fairly easy once you learn how to do it. There is a plus side in being able to make your own web updates. If a design company is going to give you *pro bono* services to help create your site and manage the graphics (which I think *is* rocket science for anyone over the age of twenty), it will be more of an incentive for them to help you if the burden of text updating is not also placed on their staff. The minus in doing those updates yourself is that it does take some time to accomplish. Considering the power of the Internet and the value of having an organizational website, however, it is time well spent. Having outdated information on your site leaves a bad impression with your visitors.

As we discussed in Chapter 10, Why Should I Evaluate My PR Efforts?, be sure to include a counter on your website so you can measure the number of "hits" (visitors) to the site. If you aren't getting much traffic, you will need to investigate why.

- Is your address too difficult?
- When people search key words, does your site come up? If not, how can you make that happen?
- Is the site boring?
- Have you given people a compelling reason to visit your site?

You may be groaning by now because this seems like such a daunting task. Take heart. It really is worth all the effort. A website will allow your organization to have an ongoing dialogue with your audience. It will give your agency the ability to spread information to the global community and, so far, it is a cost-effective way to communicate.

There are changes coming rapidly in this exploding technology. In the future, nonprofit organizations will have webmasters on staff. More and more sites will become less static, moving to more streaming media using animation, sound, and "virtual" experiences. Organizations will be using the web for advocacy issues, for efforts to promote earned

> Keep uppermost in your mind exactly what you are trying to accomplish with your website.

income programs, and to sell merchandise or hold fundraising "silent auctions." So this chapter is just the tip of the iceberg on websites. Keep your eyes and ears open and be receptive to all the new technology coming your way. The Internet is here to stay, and if you don't jump on the super highway, it may just pass you by!

What about Electronic Communications?

·16·

Now that you have your website in the works, let's talk about computers, e-mail, faxes, and cell phones. This technology is changing so rapidly that it can be a challenge just to know what digital TV and high-definition TV mean! However, technology is also quickly becoming the PR person's best friend.

In the early 1980s, I ran a satellite special projects office for the National League of POW/MIA Families. I communicated by phone and mail with the families, veterans groups, and concerned citizens working for an accounting of those people still listed as prisoner of war and missing in action in Southeast Asia as a result of the Vietnam War. I coordinated projects they could implement in their own communities to keep public awareness about the issue high.

My trusty old typewriter cranked out twenty to thirty letters a day, each one individually typed. A family friend had just started selling computers and couldn't believe I didn't have one. He arranged to have a computer donated to the organization. It took a while, but once I had mastered the original Word Star program and negotiating in DOS, I was able to triple my effectiveness. Today, mastering a computer is so much easier—my mother searches the Net and e-mails my siblings. PCs became a much better tool for ordinary people when they borrowed the icon system from Macs and understanding DOS was no longer necessary for most people to use their computers.

Computers are marvelous tools for increasing productivity and, for the PR staff, are essential for effectively communicating the mission, services, goals, and needs of your organization. Computers are becoming less expensive and easier to operate. But for some nonprofits, having good basic computers and printers available for most staff members can be difficult because of budget constraints.

How Do You Get Computers?

There are many organizations, like major accounting firms, advertising agencies, and banks, that upgrade their computers every year or two. These businesses are usually happy to donate their old computers to worthy nonprofits. In some cases, computer makers will donate both hardware (the computer hard drive, monitor, keyboard, and printer) and software (the programs that are loaded onto the hard drive). You need to do some homework to find out which firms donate computers and if your agency is a fit with their philanthropic mission. For example, IBM has made a substantial commitment to support kindergarten through twelfth grade education in communities across the country. If your agency works in an area that helps further that mission, IBM might consider a donation of new or reconditioned equipment—and the expertise of an IBM staff member to help you set things up. If a local bank supports the arts as a corporate goal, your theater company's office staff may be the recipient of donated recycled computers.

Another avenue is to get on the Internet and search for the keywords "free computer." You may be surprised at what you find. Just be careful and make sure offers for free computers are legitimate and you don't get scammed.

Don't Forget about Printers

There is really no bigger waste of employee time than for staff members (who may actually have decent computers) to all share one laser printer that is located down the hall. To print on agency letterhead, you have to trek down the hall to put the paper in the printer (hopefully the right way!), tell the other staffers not to print for a few minutes, and then scoot back to your cubicle to press the "print" button. The time saved by using the computer is eaten up by the logistics needed just to be able to print out the information. The price of good-quality printers for normal correspondence and reports has become very reasonable.

If efforts to have computers and printers donated don't pan out, go to a computer retailer and negotiate a deep discount for the agency. Computer prices have fallen into a range where purchasing one really good computer and printer for the public relations staff person need not be unrealistic.

Connect to the Internet

At the very least, the PR staff should have a computer that is connected to the Internet. Check with Internet providers to see if they can provide that service free of charge to your nonprofit organization. If you don't know any Internet providers, ask friends and associates who are

Investigate ways to get free computers for your nonprofit.

computer-savvy. Having Internet access allows you to constantly monitor your agency's website to ensure it is kept up-to-date. You can also use the Internet for research. For example, a small agency that plants trees at schools and public parks wants to expand the variety of trees it provides. Jumping on the Internet, the staff are able to find a different species that can thrive in the local climate. Information about the new tree becomes the basis for a news story on "The New Tree in Town," which helps recruit more volunteer tree-planters and generates more donations to purchase the new trees.

E-Mail: the Good, the Bad, and the Ugly

Being connected to the Internet also means you can take advantage of electronic mail. E-mail is a wonderful thing—its uses are endless:

- Pitch stories to reporters
- Communicate with your board of directors
- Confirm appointments

You can also attach documents to your e-mails. If you have a story that needs to be reviewed by someone outside the office, you can send it to his or her computer as an attachment. Be aware, however, that many people will not accept e-mail attachments because they use software programs that are different from the one used to create the attachment and they can't open it. There is also some justifiable concern about importing a virus into their own computer system from an e-mail or an attachment. Consider asking people in your e-mail address book if they want to receive attachments. If they don't, simply cut the attachment copy and paste it into your e-mail.

There are some downsides to e-mail. The virus concern is very real. Installing an anti-virus program on your computer will help screen for them. E-mail is also about as private as sending a postcard to someone. If you don't want to share the information you are sending with anyone but the recipient, don't send it in an e-mail. E-mail advertisements can also be annoying. I simply delete these without reading them and get on with reading, responding to, and sending out necessary and productive e-mail for my job. If electronic junk mail really irritates you, investigate services or software programs to screen them out. And then there are the endless jokes some people feel compelled to forward to everyone they know. Hopefully, "computer funnies" will go the way of CB radios, 8-track tapes, and disco dancing!

Faxes

Your computer can also be used to fax information. There is now technology available so you can fax, copy, and e-mail from the same machine. Using faxes can be a marvelous way to communicate quickly. However, as discussed in Chapter 4, Why Must I Have Media Relations?, faxing press releases is probably not the best way to get information placed. It is usually difficult to get through to a television station or newspaper's fax machine, and often your fax never actually gets to the person who needs to see it. The other point to remember about faxing is that your communication is not private. Don't fax sensitive information.

Using the fax machine to communicate quickly with your board of directors is a good idea. If your agency is involved in some kind of bill before the state legislature, you can fax board members copies of the bill or proposed changes and ask them to contact their representative to urge them to vote on the bill. But don't fax confidential financial information to the board.

Cell Phones

Cell phones are also good communication tools. Most phones are now equipped with the ability to take voice mail messages and store frequently used numbers. The phones are so small they can fit in your pocket, and costs can be kept very reasonable. Having a portable phone lets you communicate away from the office. By checking your office voice mail, you can respond to media inquiries in a more timely manner. You can alert appointments if you get stuck in traffic. Think about how accessible you want to be, however. Is it really necessary to leave your cell phone on all the time? If you are at a lunch meeting with a potential sponsor, do you really want your cell phone ringing in your pocket? And don't forget the safety issues of talking on a cell phone while driving a car.

Digital Cameras

A digital camera is another useful little electronic device. It has the advantage of allowing you to view instantly the photograph you have taken so you can delete it and reshoot if the shot wasn't exactly what you wanted. You can print out copies of the photos from your computer, post them on your website, or e-mail them to a reporter as part of a pitch.

A digital camera is a great tool for a nonprofit PR staff person. Just think, you don't have to wait to see if that shot you took of Mary the volunteer at the fall bazaar is as good as you thought, or if Mary is standing in front of a display of laser swords and it looks like a broom is growing out of her head!

> Remember that e-mails and faxes are not private forms of communication. Never e-mail or fax sensitive information.

There is no way to predict what technological marvels will emerge in the future. Like e-mail, fax machines, computer calendars, electronic notebooks, and palm-size systems that do it all (which so many people depend on today), there will be even more innovations that will make your ability to communicate for your nonprofit even more effective. Being receptive to new technology will always give you an edge. Obtaining that technology inexpensively for your organization is even better.

■ Being receptive to new technology will always give you an edge.

What Is Networking and Why Should I?

·17·

This chapter will not help you learn about linking computers together in a network. Business networking is not about computers; it is about people. It is placing yourself in situations where you can meet many types of people to build contacts that will benefit both parties through a sharing of knowledge and resources. It is not selling. It is relationship-building that helps you increase your ability to do your job. Networking is a process that is an essential part of a good public relations program.

Where to Begin?

The opportunities to network are all around you.

- A good place to start is by joining your local public relations association and attending as many of the monthly meetings as possible. As a member, you should also receive invitations to other functions held by advertising agencies, television stations, public relations firms, and other charities. Attend all the events you can so you meet people who can share their PR successes and challenges with you.
- Join the local press club and attend meetings to interact with reporters and assignment editors.
- Network at high school and college reunions, community or professional organization meetings, and conventions.

Okay, I can hear a chorus of voices protesting: "I don't have time;" "I don't need to meet people outside my agency's field of expertise;" "I'm too shy." Aha! Shyness is the main reason most people stay away from many of the social situations that could give them opportunities to tell people about their charitable organization. These are also excellent places to meet new friends, learn about other businesses and organizations, and pick up tips on strategies and programs that might translate well into your agency.

Just as corporate CEOs and business executives use this skill routinely, everyone in the nonprofit sector needs to learn the power of networking. Try to overcome the uncomfortable feeling of walking into a large meeting or social gathering where you don't know anyone by setting small goals for yourself. Vow to walk up to one person and introduce yourself. Chances are that person is also feeling awkward. Say something like, "I'm Jane Doe with Save the Snails. I don't know anyone here. Do you?" Or try, "Hello, I'm Jane Doe with Save the Snails. Tell me about your organization." Be interested, positive, and upbeat, and project a sense of humor. Engage in small talk, which is a form of communication that is nonthreatening but informational. And don't forget to listen when others are talking. That sounds simple but can sometimes be difficult if you are worrying about what people think of you or pondering what you will say next.

Share Networking Ideas with Other Nonprofits
A good way to avoid some of the pressures of attending a function where you don't know anyone is to network by initiating regular gatherings with people who handle communication/public relations duties at other nonprofit agencies. Meet monthly or quarterly for a brown bag lunch at one member's location. Talk about ideas for sharing resources such as media lists, the names of good freelance writers, or outstanding printers.

While at the science museum, I belonged to a group that called itself the Big 8 Marketing Group. The marketing directors from eight cultural attractions in the city met on a fairly regular basis to share ideas and explore ways to market the attractions, which ranged from the zoo to an art museum. While in some ways all eight organizations were competing for visitors, we found that cooperation actually netted everyone more attendance.

> Initiate regular gatherings with people who handle PR duties at other nonprofits.

We shared marketing tips, pooled money for joint advertising, and tried packaging visits to several of our institutions to offer to tour operators. We also helped each other in times of "challenges." One day my counterpart at the zoo called and told me that there was a water main break and they had to close the zoo because all the toilets and drinking fountains were nonfunctional. She had three buses from out of state rolling in for a school field trip. Could my museum take them? We took in this group—at the zoo's group rate, which was lower than ours. However, we also exposed a new school system to our facility, which they had never visited before. So it really was a win-win situation for both organizations—and it came about through networking.

When you do attend networking events, take plenty of business cards. Exchange cards with people to build a Rolodex that includes a wide variety of people who can help you access information and resources that you may need in the future. The public relations director of a local furniture store will be able to tell you how to go about soliciting the company for a donation to the silent auction at your agency's annual black tie fundraising gala. A chiropractor might be willing to talk about providing free adjustments after your annual sports day for fathers and sons. A hotel sales and catering manager can help you figure out a budget for feeding one hundred people at an educational luncheon. You get the idea.

Follow-up Is Important

At the beginning of this chapter, I stated that networking is a process. It is more than just meeting people at a function and exchanging business cards. Following up after the initial meeting and staying in touch are also important parts of that process. Within a week of meeting a new contact, call or e-mail that person.

- Help solidify a new relationship by scheduling a breakfast or lunch meeting to talk about the challenges each of you faces and how you might support each other.
- Contact someone you haven't talked to for a while. Perhaps that person has been involved with a new project and hasn't had time to do anything but deal with deadlines. Call with a compliment on how well the publicity for the project went and offer understanding of the amount of work that went into it.
- Call a contact for help. I needed the name of a youngster killed in a plane crash four years earlier for a story I was writing. I called a reporter friend at the local newspaper. In ten minutes he had located the story in the paper's archives and e-mailed the information to me. A few days later, he asked me to read a column he was writing. He needed a "gut" reaction from someone who wasn't as close to (or knowledgeable about) the information as he was. We were being mutually supportive resources for each other.
- Mail notes or cards to new contacts—invite them to your special events.
- Think about who in your network might be with an organization that would be appropriate to link to your agency's website.

Always have plenty of business cards on hand. ■

Networking does require a time commitment, and most nonprofit organizations find their employees stretched pretty thinly already. However, it is important that your executive director (who should also be networking) support this kind of activity. The benefits are enormous.

A list of professional organizations is included in the appendix. These groups can tell you about meetings in your area. Start attending now and join if you can. Just get out there and network! You will realize the benefits almost immediately.

RATE YOUR NETWORKING SKILLS

A "yes" or "no" to each statement will give you a networking skills rating:

1. At my organization's last social event, I started a conversation with someone I didn't know.
2. I often say "hello" to people I don't know when I'm waiting in line.
3. I always carry my business cards with me, even on vacation.
4. I initiate follow-up with people I meet.
5. I send holiday cards to my networking contacts.
6. I belong to a professional organization and I've volunteered to serve on its committees.
7. I've volunteered to speak at a meeting of my professional organization.
8. I've submitted suggestions for improvement within my organization.

Scoring: You know how to network successfully if you said "yes" to every statement. If you said "no" to some, you're missing some good networking opportunities.

Reprinted with permission from *Communications Briefings*. Source: Barbara Pachter, Pachter & Associates, P.O. Box 3680, Cherry Hill, NJ 08034. Barbara Pachter is also the author of *When the Little Things Count . . . and They Always Count: 601 Essential Things People in Business Need to Know.* ∎

What Else?

·18·

What else could there possibly be? This chapter presents some additional public relations/marketing techniques (beyond press releases, media relations, and publications) to think about and incorporate into your nonprofit organization when resources and need dictate.

Reputation Management

One concept employed in the corporate world is something I believe has great relevance for nonprofits: reputation management. Some larger, national nonprofits have embraced reputation management for years and may not even have known that's what they were doing. It has to do with the credibility and perception of professionalism of the organization. Your agency's reputation is its most important asset.

A nonprofit's reputation is formed by many things. Everything affects how the public perceives the professionalism and effectiveness of your agency, from the way your publications look to how the staff handles telephone inquiries and how much of each dollar raised is spent on administrative costs. Creating and maintaining a good reputation is vital for the health of nonprofit organizations. Since the public relations staff person is usually the one who ends up having to "fix things" when there is a reputation problem, it is in your best interest—and that of your agency—to always keep reputation management in mind.

The first step is to determine just what the public perception of your agency is. Gather information from the general public (and from your specific audiences) on impressions they have about the organization: services, employees, and financial management. Where did people get these impressions—from the media, word of mouth, reading your publications, or visiting your website?

When goals and objectives for the agency are being created or revised, provide input that will help keep reputation management as a priority for all staff and volunteers. Remind the board of directors and the executive director that a commitment to maintaining a good reputation is essential and can be achieved by routinely reviewing the agency's actions to ensure that its mission and goals are being fulfilled. Encourage all of the agency's employees to buy into the mission. At some nonprofits, "territorialism" runs rampant. The education program staff constantly "competes" with the client services staff and the resulting friction is obvious to the organization's public. It is important for staff members to remember that they all belong to the same organization and that the mission and goals are the same for each program within the agency.

Reputation management is a daily, hourly building process. It is everyone's job because the actions of each staff member and volunteer impact the organization's reputation. There are books on this topic, and although they relate mostly to the corporate world, it might be worth your time to review them. Go to the Internet and search for the keywords "reputation management" through any of the online booksellers. You will probably also find public relations firms on the web that offer reputation management consultation. That is an expensive service and one I believe most small nonprofits don't need unless there is a major problem. Doing some research and understanding the need to keep your agency's good name unsoiled should suffice.

The credibility of an agency is based on everyday performance. Never lose sight of that basic fact. Help create a system that will ensure that all agency staff and volunteers take personal pride in accomplishing the mission of the agency and are dedicated to administering public funds honestly and carefully. This will ensure that the reputation of your nonprofit organization will be sterling.

> Never lose sight of this basic fact: the credibility of an agency is based on everyday performance.

Using PR Interns Effectively

Many colleges and universities offer internships through their public relations or communications departments. A typical internship lasts for a school quarter or semester, with the students receiving school credit. The nonprofit agency is responsible for filling out some paperwork from the school to evaluate the intern's progress and for detailing the duties assigned to him or her. To find out more about student interns, contact colleges or universities in your area to find the person in the public relations or communications department responsible for overseeing internships. I say "in your area," but don't limit yourself. If there is a university 150 miles from your town or city that has a good communications department, there may be students who haven't been able to find a slot locally or who have a preference to work in your geographical area or in the field your organization covers. Maybe yours is a child-serving agency and there is a student who is especially interested in focusing his or her career on helping children.

There are other people who eagerly seek out public relations internships as well:

- College graduates trying to determine which area of PR/communications/marketing is right for them
- An older person wanting to make a career change
- A stay-at-home mom ready to get back into the PR field after raising a family

To locate these kinds of interns, a small classified ad in the employment section of the newspaper is often effective. Or, if you are in an area with an active chapter of the Public Relations Society of America, check to see if you can list your internship availability in their member newsletter or on their website.

In the past, internships at nonprofits were usually nonpaying positions. That has changed in many areas of the country. Typically, an intern is paid a small stipend for the length of the internship (usually two to four months). It is often easier to find a good intern if there is some money involved. (While this doesn't apply to most nonprofits, there was a case in the 1990s where a public relations agency was billing a client at the usual agency rate for work performed by an unpaid intern. The client discovered this information and sued the agency. After that lawsuit, most nonprofits in the region began offering a stipend just to be absolutely sure they were within legal boundaries. However, some nonprofits simply called their interns "volunteers" and continued to function on a no-fee basis.)

Let's discuss what kind of work your intern will perform. Obviously, this is supposed to be a learning experience for the intern and, as such, students should be provided the opportunity to do things that will help them grow in their chosen profession. The usual tasks that come to mind for interns are stuffing and sticking labels on envelopes, faxing, copying, collating, and telephoning. It's perfectly okay to ask interns to do those tasks—heck, we all have to do those things, right? But it isn't all right to make those the only chores your intern performs. That defeats the purpose of the internship.

Make an effort to include your intern in all aspects of your public relations activities:

- Give the intern the chance to write a calendar notice or press release, submit it to the local newspaper, and then use any resulting coverage for his or her portfolio.

- Allow the student to work on your quarterly newsletter or produce your annual conference's "Save the Date" postcard. (Yeah, yeah, so you'll need to spend a little more time guiding the process and you'll probably feel that it's easier just to do it yourself. But consider the time you spend helping your intern learn as a payoff for the time you didn't have to copy or collate a project your intern completed.)
- Provide opportunities for your intern to participate in planning meetings for special events. He or she may have a fresh idea no one else has thought about.
- Let interns help with media when there is coverage of an event. Learning how to deal with a camera crew tromping around looking for the perfect visual and sound bite can be a valuable lesson for a PR intern.

Always treat your interns with dignity and respect. Remember that you are (for the length of their internship) their teacher. Sometimes, your role is to help them understand their limitations. You will find that some students (and some older folks) who really have the desire to work in the public relations area prove over and over again that it is not the field for them. I had an intern one time who couldn't write his way out of a paper sack and hated what he called the "mundane" tasks. But when we were desperately searching for a Santa Claus for a huge special event, he volunteered and did a masterful job. He intuitively understood the need to establish a flow of children and suggested there be a Polaroid camera to take photos for children whose parents didn't have a camera. This young man needed to shift his focus to the event planning side.

Another important point to remember is that interns are not your excuse. How many times have I been tempted to cover a mistake I made by saying, "You know, my intern was supposed to fax that to you and must have forgotten." Wrong! I'm the one who forgot. Don't get into the habit of blaming your intern for goof-ups—not only because it isn't fair to the intern, but also because we all have to learn to accept responsibility for our own mistakes.

Public relations interns are a tremendous resource for nonprofit organizations that have limited PR staff capabilities. They can vastly expand your ability to communicate with your all-important public. They also bring a fresh eye to your agency. If you have been communicating the message for Save the Snails for three years and just don't have any new ideas, an intern may provide that spark that gets you out of the box and back on track creatively.

Interns are a tremendous resource for nonprofits with limited PR staff capabilities.

Exhibits and Displays

Having a first-rate display or mini-exhibit is an outstanding way to promote your agency's mission. This is one area where, again, you really don't want to be "penny-wise and pound-foolish." A well-designed, easy-to-transport display unit that is not difficult to set up is well worth the investment. And this is another opportunity to look for a corporate sponsor. Try to find a display design company that will provide a discount or donate work in exchange for marketing opportunities such as:

- Signage on the display or exhibit unit
- Appropriate acknowledgment of the display company's assistance in your agency's publications
- The ability to place information about their company in front of your constituents

The challenge for many nonprofit organizations is to resist the temptation to make their own displays. The end product usually looks just like what it is—homemade! Not that there is anything wrong with that, but it probably won't communicate the seriousness and professionalism of the agency as effectively as a professional display.

For example, when I worked for a child abuse prevention organization, the display was a three-fold tabletop unit with brochures and information on the seven programs and services offered by the agency mounted on the panels. The display had too much information posted on it, which resulted in overloading and intimidating people. I was fortunate to find a local company willing to donate a new display to the organization. Their initial assessment was that we were basically trying to tell people viewing our display everything about the organization on three panels. They also observed that many people are hesitant to visit a booth or display that screamed child abuse from so many pamphlets. Their goal was to create a display that would compel people to visit the booth and then staff and volunteers could provide more specific, targeted information for each person.

The design company accomplished their goal by using a photograph of a five-year-old child. The photo had been produced for the agency's annual report. The girl's big, beautiful eyes dominated the shot. Superimposed over the photo was an image of broken glass, so it appeared as if the child was looking through shattered glass. That photo was enlarged to fit on a free-standing display unit that could also be configured for tabletop use. The agency's name was placed on a header that topped the unit. The other panels had more photos and limited label copy. The display dominated the exhibit area wherever it went. People were drawn to it and once they came to the booth to examine it, admire it, or ask who the child was, they were over that hesitation most people have about seeking out a booth related to child abuse. The display was different, attention-grabbing, and communicated volumes. That is what you need to find for your organization. It doesn't have to be expensive—just unique and different.

Think about where your agency might use a display or exhibit effectively. Come on, now; get out of that nonprofit box.

- You are a small agency that provides free tutoring for disadvantaged children. There is a computer trade show in town. Ask for free booth space. Take your fabulous display and some of your computers and load them with cool software for kids and parents to access. You'll get lots of opportunities to educate people about your service, and—who knows?—maybe one of the computer companies displaying at the show will see how woefully your agency is in need of new computers and donate them to you!

- Ask a car dealership if you can set up your display on a weekend when they are promoting a sale. See if they will also donate one or two percent of each car sold that weekend to your cause.

- A new Wal-Mart is opening in your community. Request space for your display and offer to have one or two simple techniques available to show kids (and their parents!) how to solve some of the most troubling math problems. Offer "tricks of the trade" for remembering how to spell difficult words and demonstrate how a computer's spell check doesn't always do the trick.

A Georgia-based organization honoring women who made significant contributions in their field made a small traveling exhibit on their honorees available for a small fee to schools, churches, and museums. It was on display in the state capitol building while the state legislature was in session. That's an incredible way to get your message in front of lawmakers for advocacy purposes. The display will also be seen by the many schoolchildren on field trips and other visitors to a state capitol building.

The basic idea for any display or exhibit is to have a vehicle for public awareness about your organization and/or cause that will impact large numbers of people in a short period of time. Having access to the ten thousand people who attend a local home and garden show gives your organization faster exposure than speaking to every Rotary Club in the state over the course of a year. Put careful thought and resources into this kind of public relations tool.

Put careful thought and resources into creating displays and deciding the best places to use them.

Branding

Branding is one of those "buzzwords" that you suddenly start hearing and most people have no clue of its meaning. Branding has been around for years. A good way to explain it is to ask these questions: When you need to blow your nose, do you ask for a tissue or for a Kleenex? When you need to photocopy something, do you copy it or Xerox it? Because of those companies' branding efforts, their products' names have become synonymous with the products.

So, starting from there, why would a nonprofit organization want to be involved in any kind of branding campaign? I suppose the answer to that question will depend greatly on the mission of your organization. If you are an art museum, you want to be branded as a "must see" so people will think about bringing out-of-town visitors to your venue. If you are a homeless shelter, you want caterers, hotels, and meeting planners to donate leftover food for your clients. You want people in the wedding party that ended up with too much food to know exactly who you are so they donate all of that expensive leftover food to a good cause (instead of putting it all in baggies to cart home).

I am going to give you some thoughts on how to market (or brand) your agency. And I know for certain that I will hear from others in my profession about how I am using the term incorrectly and that what I suggest is really marketing or public relations or community relations. Okay, fine. But for your purposes, it doesn't matter if the activity fits into the proper niche. What matters is that you market your brand in your community so people will know who you are, use your services, sign up as volunteers, and donate money.

My concept of branding for small nonprofits is to augment other public relations activities. Listed below are some ideas. You can expand upon that list and do what you are able to do within the confines of your budget, volunteer resources, and comfort level in begging for donations of goods and services.

- The obvious: T-shirts, bumper stickers, and ball caps. The trick here is to create a good slogan so people will display these items. The history center's slogan was "We Keep History from Getting Old." The zoo's bumper sticker declared "You Belong in the Zoo." The child abuse agency used "No One Beats Our Kids." And the interactive science museum touted "Science You Can Handle." Have all staff and volunteers that deal with the public wear your agency shirts.
- Less obvious: Specialty items like refrigerator magnets, pencils, and bookmarks. Think of creative ways to distribute these items. Have

a good vinyl banner made and hang it from your building or on a bridge crossing over the interstate. If some of your volunteers are going to New York to shop and see plays, send a banner with them and task them with standing outside *The Today Show* studio with the banner!

The idea of branding is to have your organization's name and logo in front of as many people as possible. The more familiar people are with a name, the more credibility they will usually give it.

Finally

The final "What Else?" is simply a personal note. Public relations is a challenging and satisfying career. If you decide it is your path, jump in with both feet and do it! Never stop listening and learning, and never compromise your integrity. Remember that while you try to be perfect, mistakes happen. Fix them or apologize for them and go on. Enjoy what I believe is the most rewarding, challenging, demanding, misunderstood, and fun job in the world.

Why Should I Ask My Boss to Read This Chapter?

·19·

You should ask your boss to read this chapter because it will make your job easier! Mark these pages and leave them in your boss's chair, where it will be obvious this is something that needs attention now. Actually, it would be better if he or she would read the entire book, but knowing how busy most nonprofit executive directors are, that may be impossible.

The reason I want the head of a nonprofit agency to read this chapter is to be sure the person who supervises the public relations staff understands where these new ideas are coming from. There is no point in getting the communications staff person cranked up and excited about getting out there to raise the agency above the fold if the boss isn't also "buying into" the program.

In the twenty-first century, we are way beyond the days when a charitable organization could expect support and volunteers just because they were doing good works. Too many things have changed.

As of the writing of this book, there are over fourteen thousand registered nonprofits in the state of Georgia alone. That's a lot of good causes trying to attract money and support. Nonprofits are now in a situation where they have—heaven help us—*competition* for the public's interest, donations, support, and time. In so many families today both parents work. The former supply of stay-at-home mom volunteers has almost dried up. Corporations no longer want to write a check, have a "grip and grin" photo in the local paper, and feel good about their contribution. They want marketing benefits for their money.

So what's a poor nonprofit to do? Act like a business! I am probably "preaching to the choir" here for many of you but certainly not for all. There are still plenty of agencies that are drowning in the old nonprofit mindset: "We have always done it that way." "We can't advertise." "We don't need public relations."

Every nonprofit organization on the face of the earth needs public relations in some form or another. As I stated in the introduction to this book, public relations is not a dirty word. It is a useful, practical, and necessary part of the business of nonprofit agencies in the twenty-first century. Allowing your organization's communications staff to function within the parameters of how good PR is practiced is essential.

Successful public relations is not practiced by having someone sit at a desk all day pounding out updates for your board of directors on how many clients you served. Perhaps that is part of your communications program, but it may be a function that another staff member can help accomplish while your PR staffer is attending a networking luncheon.

Your support of the person you designate to handle public relations duties is essential for your agency to reap the full benefits of a PR program. You must be receptive to making sure that staff person has the tools for the job. One of the most important tools is his or her title. "Communications Coordinator" is a very dated term. It communicates "nonprofit organization afraid to use the words 'public relations.'" Be brave. Have a "public relations/marketing director" (or manager or coordinator—whichever best fits the hierarchy of titles in your organization).

> Your support of the person you designate to handle public relations duties is essential for your agency to reap the full benefits of a PR program.

Once you have assigned a title to your staff person, be sure to have business cards printed in ample supply. This is not a huge expense and your PR person is going to look so stupid in the real world without business cards. Can you afford to have a direct telephone line for your public relations office? This is really a help for media calls—especially if your agency has the voice-mail menu from hell. A direct line can have very specific information for media on its voice message, directing callers to another person if the PR staff member is not at her phone and the media representative is on deadline and needs an answer now.

Be receptive to professional development opportunities for your public relations person.

- Is there any way to allow him or her to attend seminars or workshops on media relations, reputation management, annual report writing, or sponsorship opportunities? The benefits may translate into major donations of money or in-kind services.

- Does your PR person have some level of decision-making ability? How comfortable are you in letting that staff member represent the agency at a meeting with other organizations where a collaborative effort is being crafted to create joint sponsorships of your programs? Have you had a discussion with him or her on exactly what decisions can be made independently and which ones need to be cleared by you or the board of directors?

• Are you accessible to your PR person if the media call wanting a comment for the evening news? Have you allowed media-training sessions for agency staff and have you participated in that training yourself? Are you willing to go the extra mile and be at the television studio at 6:00 A.M. with a volunteer to be on the local morning talk show?

These are all important things to remember because if you aren't in this kind of mindset, it doesn't matter how good your public relations staff person is. Your lack of cooperation could put roadblocks in the way.

With the support and cooperation of you and the board of directors, an energetic, enthusiastic, hardworking public relations staff person (who is willing to learn and is not afraid to go where some nonprofits have not gone before) can accomplish tremendous things for your agency. You need to be flexible, cooperative, understanding, supportive, and receptive to new ways of communicating. Your public relations staff person should be an important part of the management team of your organization.

You need to be flexible, cooperative, understanding, supportive, and receptive to new ways of communicating.

Additional Resources

American Jewish Press Association
www.ajpa.org
(This site lists Jewish publications and freelance writers.)

American Society of Association Executives
1575 1st St., NW
Washington, DC 20005
202-626-2723
www.asaenet.org

Association for Women in Communications
780 Ritchie Highway, Suite 28S
Severna, MD 21146
410-544-7442
www.womcom.org

Canadian Public Relations Society
277 Richmond St., W.
Toronto, Ontario, M5V 1X1
416-597-0188
www.cprs.ca

Center for Communication
271 Madison Ave., Suite 700
New York, NY 10016
www.cencom.org

Florida Public Relations Association
73 S. Palm Ave., Suite 223
Sarasota, FL 34236
941-365-2135
www.fpra.org

International Association of Business Communicators
One Hallidie Plaza, Suite 600
San Francisco, CA 94102
415-544-4700
www.iabc.com

The Institute for Public Relations
University of Florida
P.O. Box 118400
Gainesville, FL 32611-8400
352-392-0280
www.instituteforpr.com

National Association of Government Communicators
10301 Democracy Lane, Suite 203
Fairfax, VA 27030
703-691-0377
www.nagc.com

National Association of Science Writers
P.O. Box 294
Greenlawn, NY 11740
631-757-5664
www.nasw.org

National Black Public Relations Society
6565 Sunset Blvd., Suite 301
Hollywood, CA 90028
323-466-8221
www.nbprs.org

National Catholic Association for
    Communicators
701 Irving Avenue
Dayton, OH 45409
937-229-2303
www.undausa.org

National School Public Relations Association
15948 Denwood Road
Rockville, MD 20855
301-519-0496
www.nspra.org

Nonprofit Resource Center
www.not-for-profit.org
(Search for the center in your state using keywords "nonprofit resource center in [state].")

North Carolina Association of Government
    Information Officers
P.O. Box 25533
Raleigh, NC 27611-5533
www.geocities.com

Public Communicators of Los Angeles
1910 West Sunset Blvd., Suite 860
Los Angeles, CA 90026
213-387-PCLA
www.pcla.org

Public Relations Society of America
33 Irving Place, 3rd Floor
New York, NY 10003-2376
212-995-2230
www.prsa.org
(This site can link you to local PRSA chapters.)

Publicity Club of Chicago
875 North Michigan Ave., Suite 2250
Chicago, IL 60611
312-640-6725
www.publicity.org

The Religion Communicators Council
475 Riverside Drive
Suite 1948 A
New York, NY 10115
212-870-2985
www.religioncommunicators.org

Southern Public Relations Federation
www.sprf.org
(This site will link you to its members, including
the Public Relations Council of Alabama, the
Public Relations Association of Louisiana, the
Emerald Coast Public Relations Organization,
and the Public Relations Association of
Mississippi.)

Texas Public Relations Association
P.O. Box 6496
Corpus Christi, TX 78466
1-800-525-0405
www.tpra.org

www.tech.prsa.org/journal.html
(This listing has excellent links to news and
media organizations.)

Index
